Another Word for Love

Another Word
for Love a memoir

Carvell Wallace

MCD FARRAR, STRAUS AND GIROUX NEW YORK

MCD
Farrar, Straus and Giroux
120 Broadway, New York 10271

Printed in the United States of America
First edition, 2024

Frontispiece photograph courtesy of the author.

Library of Congress Control Number: 2023050756
ISBN: 978-0-374-23782-0

Designed by Abby Kagan

Our books may be purchased in bulk for promotional, educational, or business use. Please contact your local bookseller or the Macmillan Corporate and Premium Sales Department at 1-800-221-7945, extension 5442, or by email at MacmillanSpecialMarkets@macmillan.com.

www.mcdbooks.com • www.fsgbooks.com
Follow us on social media at @mcdbooks and @fsgbooks

10 9 8 7 6 5 4 3 2 1

For Julie Moon

thin skin protects the part
that dulls from longing

—June Jordan, "Who Look at Me"

Some names and details have been slightly altered to protect, care for, and love the people who have protected, cared for, and loved me.

Contents

Part One: Stories About Loss

The Quiet   3

The Fog   6

The Snow   9

The Razors   17

The Boys   19

The Everything   24

The Clothes   31

The Music   34

The Police   45

The Finger   50

The Police Again   54

The Smoke   61

The Birth   66

The End   70

The Death   73

Part Two: Stories About God

The Journalist   81

The Moon   87

The Lightning   91

Part Three: Stories About Reunion

The Stars   95

The Quit   105

The Universe   115

The Pandemic   122

The Plants   128

The End Again   132

The Bread   146

The Beauty   154

The Sex   159

The Touch   171

The No   187

The Love   194

The Mother   203

The Winner II   220

The Dog   226

The Rain   235

Postscript: A Story About Dill

The Dill   245

Acknowledgments   251

Part One

Stories About Loss

The Quiet

We had been homeless for about a year. We never slept on the street; mostly we bounced from one temporary living situation to another with the occasional night in a motel or a car. Some of these situations were fine. Some were not. Maybe it was less than a year but it felt like a long time, full of endings and tiny deaths.

I was seven and a half years old, almost eight. We eventually found an apartment in Virginia, which I could tell meant a lot to my mother. There was one bedroom, a small patio, a kitchen, and a sunken living room, which I guessed was a thing to be coveted by the reverence with which these words—"sunken living room"—were spoken.

I remember the days in that apartment as lonely ones. It was just the two of us. The afternoons were long and quiet. We had no furniture, save for a bunk bed and a rocking chair whose lengthening shadow would spread across my body as I lay on the empty carpet while afternoon turned to night and my mother slept like she had briefly died. We had just come through a chaotic period of homelessness and now we had a place. We were tired, but our safety here was flimsy. I knew even then that eventually we would lose this place like we lost all others. We were like survivors of a shipwreck who had washed ashore onto a deserted island. We had made it, but for how long?

Food was not guaranteed. Sometimes I ate from a stick of butter when I was hungry. It gave me a headache, but I also loved the warm recklessness of it, putting something slick and salty in my mouth, a forbidden overflow of flavors that almost made me nauseated, but not quite. Other times there were restaurant leftovers. I knew my mother went on dates to get takeout for us, and I was grateful whenever I saw a noisy, oversize Styrofoam container in the fridge. Cold salty half-chewed steaks, gummy fries, rock-hard cakes, and chewy slices of garlic bread. It was like eating from a very nice trash can. I gorged myself whenever I could.

Maybe I first began to contemplate death in those afternoons of lengthening shadows. The TV would be on; the final credits would be rolling on some made-for-TV action movie. My mother would be dead to the world. I would be alone with night advancing. I would feel trapped in a space between awake and sleep, between life and death, that I found intoxicating and terrifying. It was as if I was in the presence of a holy truth: the Ending of Things, the Encroaching of Shadows; the Quiet Death of a Temporary Suburban Apartment Complex at Dusk.

But wait. Maybe that is just how I made sense of things later, after I grew up and got away from there, turned myself into a poet and writer, someone who, for whatever reason, can't resist weaving stories out of aching trails of hurt and long serpentine shadows across an empty carpet floor. Maybe what I experienced then was a feeling of abandonment that shook me to my core, made me want to cry, made me feel useless, like refuse and garbage. Maybe I just needed a hug. Maybe I just needed my mother.

It's hard to know anymore what's what. I guess that's what time does, changes the meaning of things. I try not to bother too much about figuring out which truth is the truest. A lot of things, I have learned, can be true at once. That is how I have survived.

The Fog

One day around then, I was late to school, and it was a foggy morning. Usually, I walked to school, but that day my mother drove me and dropped me off at the sidewalk by the field that led to the side entrance, which was the only entrance that was open after school started. The field was huge, and the fog was so thick that you could not see the door. You just had to trust that it was there. I told my mother that I was afraid to walk through the fog by myself, but she insisted that this was the kind of fear that it was better I learn to face. I now realize it is because this was the kind of fear she was facing all the time.

She was in her twenties, a single Black woman in the world—this world, the very same one you see before you, where they break down doors and shoot Black women in their beds, leave their bodies on the sides of roads, blame them for their failure or success in surviving or not surviving, demand of them the world, their bodies, their lives, and offer them in return missing children, empty nights, and permanently broken hearts—she was in this world, mothering, intermittently homeless, holding the hand of a growing child. She had, therefore, strong feelings about how to face fearful things.

I wanted to please her. I did not tell her that I could not do it. She let me out of the car and disappeared. I began to take tiny, timid steps across the field. I was so little that even if I had taken bold steps, they still would have been tiny and timid. The cloud was thick enough that I felt like I was walking directly and unguardedly into nothingness. This might have been the end of my life. And yet there was nowhere to escape to, no choice to do anything other than to keep going. This is a feeling I will never forget as long as I live. This is a feeling I will remember when I am dying because it was a kind of dying. When I am dying, I will say, *Oh snap, this is just like the field of fog!* I kept walking, expecting any minute to be swallowed, taken to a beyond that could mean anything for me. And an astonishing thing happened, which was that the thickest, most fearsome parts of the fog were always looming in front of me, or they were behind me, but I was never in them. No matter how far I walked, I was never entirely swallowed by the gloom. It mystified me. I made it to the entrance of the school and still the area around me was clear enough for me to see. I looked back, and what I had just walked through had been the very same thing I was most afraid of. And yet I had come through it unharmed.

This would have been a lesson in fear and faith, an allegory of nearly biblical proportions in its barefaced symbolism. *My child*, the last line would say, *when you walk by faith, I will always light the way for you*, or some shit like that. But that wasn't the lesson I took from it at the time. The lesson I took from it that day was that no matter how scary a thing was, I was going to have to be able to face it entirely alone.

The Snow

It was a year before that when I learned another important lesson: the snow doesn't care about you. At all. It would let you and your mother die right there in its arms, your bodies holding each other uselessly. The snow would have kept going. It was cruel that way, even though it was so quiet and gentle, beautiful, and white, and every Christmas we sang songs about how wonderful it was. This was one of my earliest memories of learning contradiction.

It was 1982. My mother was about twenty-seven. She had a round face. A quiet beauty, even though she talked constantly. Even though she had acne and picked at it compulsively with acrylic nails. Even though she chewed the inside of her lower lip, smoked Salems, drank Coca-Cola from the can, leaving a lipstick tattoo that smelled of rose and spit against the warm flat tin. Later, toward the first end of our time together, I would sneak sips while she napped on the one mattress we had, in the one room we had, on the one afternoon we had left. I swallowed the warm, sticky flat soda seasoned with cigarette ash because even though it was gross, it was hers. She had left it for me. And as she lay there in a sleep that Shakespeare would later teach me could be described as like unto death, I felt like that ashy flat lipstick-sticky soda might, one day, be all of her I would have left. I think I've always had a knack for knowing things like that.

Anyway, we had no place to go. My mother's sister Leora had kicked us out for some reasons that I didn't understand but that I thought might have to do with the particular way in which whisky clinking on ice in a highball glass could make Leora's words come out syrupy and cruel. I wanted to stay living there because her son, Willie J, was my best friend, and we were the same age. It would have been the perfect solution, I thought. My mother wouldn't have to worry about feeding me, which seemed a source of constant stress for her. Willie J and I could play Jackson 5 and Flying Matchbox and Paper Airplane Derby and Knee Pillow Soccer all day, eating chicken and rice and Wonder Bread with butter and sugar until we had been fully sated. But when I interrupted the fight to suggest this, which I thought was a very good idea, both my mother and Aunt Leora yelled "no!" at me in a way that still echoes in my chest forty years later.

We had no place to go, and we were in the car and it

was night and very cold and my mother had grabbed me and grabbed our stuff and led me to the car in a haste, dragging me through the snow newly fallen on the walkway. And we sat in the car parked in front of the house on a night so cold I could imagine tiny flecks of ice forming on my skin like little crystals of the flesh, and I said to my mother, "Where are we going to go?" but she did not have an answer. And she turned the key in the ignition, but the car wouldn't start. It whirred and whined and complained, but it would not start. And she turned the key back. In the silence I could still hear the echo of the yelling that had happened so suddenly just a half hour before, that had exploded from downstairs, turned into what felt like a column of flames in the stairwell. My ears were still ringing. I could see my mother's breath.

She tried the car again, held the key turned for longer. The stutter of the ignition seemed to be a joke. But she held it, waiting for it to stop fucking around and get serious. I think she knew that if she let go, we would fall into an abyss and there would be nothing left to catch us. The turning over of the engine was the only thing standing between us and the uncaring hell of all there is.

In the driver's seat she was a silhouette that I looked up to. A figure haloed in aureate gold from the streetlights. Her breath escaping her mouth and ascending to heaven like a prayer made from nothing. I knew what my job was. It was to be as little trouble as possible. It was to help figure out where we would go. It was to search my head for solutions. It was to figure out how we would eat. It was to be the best son she had ever seen.

I remember, then, the falling of her face. She had a lot of emotions, my mother. She could laugh, loudly and maniacally, when something really struck her as funny. She could become quiet and angry with a violence that always reminded me of a shark. Her voice would disappear, her lips would purse, and suddenly there would be a hand flying, a sting across my cheek that I could cool only with my tears. My mouth would fill with an agitated metallic-tasting spit. I made sure never to cry louder than the sound she had made when she hit me. It was a pact we had. Neither of us would be loud and our violence would remain a secret.

But the one thing I had never seen her do, until that night, was cry. And I remember her face falling. I remember her crumpling, at first in tiny, nearly imperceptible increments down toward the earth. But soon she was falling in chunks the size of organs, of hearts and lungs, each piece collapsing into itself like a bridge under demolition, spilling section by section into a vast ravine. She collapsed and began to weep. Her weeping turned to crying and her crying to wailing. She let her head fall with an icy thud against the cold, hard plastic of the steering wheel. Her body convulsed.

I watched her. A child alone. A mother alone. A night so cold and vast, as vast, I am sure, as any night has ever been before or since. I watched her, and I tried to become an adult. I tried to see the entire universe. I tried to make sense of this moment and all the moments there were to make sense of. I tried to think of what to do. I watched her and saw that she was separate from me. Gone from me and not accessible to me anymore. I watched her and saw that I was alone. I watched her and saw that she needed me. I watched her and saw that I was not enough.

After a moment she gathered herself, lifted her head, and said only, "Please, god." Then she turned the ignition one more time. And after the briefest of moments, after one more tiny little pause of expectation, one tiny lapse of time that threatened to rip itself into a hole as big as the universe but at the very last minute just, like, decided not to, the car started. And warmth spread from the engine all the way through the body to where we sat. My mother didn't even celebrate. She just shook her head downward at the earth, her shoulders curved and hunched.

We drove into the night. Still with no place to go, but at least with a way to get there. We drove along a highway. I watched the streetlights rushing past, growing larger, closing in on me and blinding me for just a moment only to recede again into the darkness, just in time for another one to start the same thing all over again. I loved the pattern of it. Rising and falling. Coming and going. Limitless and predictable. Every ending a beginning. As above, so below.

We pulled into a Long John Silver's parking lot. The building was a triangle, the only source of light against a blue-black sky. We sat in a booth. My mother made phone calls. I fell asleep, stretching my whole form against the cold vinyl. I could see gum under the table. When I awoke again it was after closing and the sign hanging in the doorway that read OPEN was facing inward at me. A white woman in a Long John Silver's uniform was shaking her head, whispering with my mother, who was unburdening herself and picking at her acne. Her face was dotted with dozens of these marks that she had picked at until they became black spots, each one a record of how deeply the stress of being had eaten away at her flesh. In front of me a hot chocolate in a blue paper cup had appeared.

I liked watching my mother when she thought I was asleep. It was a chance to see how it all worked. Like getting a peek backstage at Disneyland and seeing the performers smoking in costume. She was an actress to me, her performance framed by the distance between me and her. Her role: the archetype. Mother with child in an unforgiving night.

We found a place to go. It was with a boyfriend, or something like that. An older man I had met once before, who was tall and quiet with a mustache and an afro that spread out from the sides and back of his balding head like a mushroom. We arrived at his apartment complex a little while later, and my mother went around back to tap on the window of his unit. He met us out front and let us in. I remember the echo of our coats and boots in the hallway steps up to his place. His apartment smelled sharp and pungent. Not entirely safe. My mother put me to bed on his couch with a thin blanket and a pillow that smelled of Afro Sheen. Before she disappeared into the bedroom with him, she turned and gave me a look. A short, pitiful, apologetic look that has gone on and on in my mind forever and ever. *I'm sorry*, the look said. *You understand.*

The thing is, I thought I did.

The shadow of snowflakes made patterns on the wall as they danced to the earth beneath the yellowing street-lights. He had a stack of *Playboy* magazines on his glass-and-dark-wood-veneer coffee table, fanned out like cards pulled from a tarot deck.

Once, I read a story—or maybe I imagined a story—of two children ages eight and twelve discovering the dead body of the grandmother who was taking care of them. The older child, a girl, took responsibility then. Feeding her younger brother, covering the body, keeping life going, until the smell got too much, and they asked a neighbor for help. They were, of course, rescued. But I often wonder what they were rescued from. It is good, of course, if they were brought into a place of safety, steady reliable meals, home, and hopefully love and care. But somewhere in me the feeling of hurtling alone is itself the feeling of home, a human truth the size of the universe, the size of my mother and me in a motel with no future to be certain of. I would never want that for myself or for my children. I would never want that for anyone.

And yet sometimes, I want it for myself.

And yet sometimes the purity of it pulls me, holds me to a crystalline clarity, like when someone you love tells you a harsh but necessary truth.

For the life of me I cannot remember if I read about

these children, or if they came to me in a waking dream, but I think of them sometimes when I feel like crying. Children, alone, trying to understand the world, with no one to guide or protect them. They are just beings engaged in the act of trying to live.

I have to stop. You know what it is like in the brain on a thing like this, the violent gale of stories churning on one another. You know how poetry is, how death and life are. How everything is. The silent spells between the ideas, the distance from one thought to the next, the unbroken space where entire gilded empires lay hushed and unspoken of.

The Razors

This is what I mean by some situations were good and some were not: On a Saturday morning when all the adults were sleeping, he took a razor and cut me with it. I bled. He told me he would cut me again if I didn't do what he wanted.

So, I did. It was so weird because I was so scared. It was so weird because I felt so small. It was weird because I was so small. In a downstairs bathroom, bleeding from the hand, a penis in my mouth, my ears ringing from where I had been punched. I felt so small. I was in a world with absolutely zero help. I felt so small. In a world where my mother slept two rooms over a million miles away and the birds that chirped outside the tiny bathroom window were unable to save me, I felt so small. The world collapses and so does time. Now and forever are one. Two rooms and a million miles are the same. You are so alone.

It was my fault, I thought. If I could fight, it wouldn't have happened. If I was bigger, it wouldn't have happened. If I was less soft, it wouldn't have happened. If I was less poor, it wouldn't have happened. If my life was different, if I were different, it wouldn't have happened. It was my fault for being the way that I am. Even though it is not my fault that I am the way that I am. Still, somehow, it is.

The Boys

When I was a child, I resented my body because it
stood in the way of my happiness. It felt wrong. It was
not fast enough or strong enough or coordinated enough
for me to have the joy of being respected and revered by
other boys. My body betrayed me by having a small blad-
der or slow hands, or by being uniquely susceptible to
pain. One of my early body memories is of the time we
were playing wiffle ball in my half brother's backyard
and I fell into a bush of thorns. My skin ripped; I was
afraid to move. I screamed and cried. My half brother,
who was only five months older than me, vacillated between trying to help me and trying not to laugh at the
delirious way I panicked, screaming for help from God
or mothers, or really anyone within a one-block radius.
Even though we couldn't have been more than six years

old, we already knew that to scream in agony was an embarrassment. We knew that bleeding was one thing, but fear was to be contained.

By the time I was in eighth grade I was holding a knife over my stomach contemplating which parts I should cut in order to appear thin and therefore more manly. The idea was that I would be scarred but I would also have a flat stomach, which would mean that I would be beautiful or at least that I would have what I thought beauty gave me: Power and respect. An ability to be unbothered. Humanity. My body was all wrong for me. It had curves and softness, my eyes were too big, my hands too delicate, my chin not rigid enough. I wanted to change these things, and if it took some knives and blood to do that, then that was what it would take. No pain, no gain. I made precisely one incision into my flesh before the sight of blood convinced me that this was a terrible idea. I covered the wound with a paper towel, thoroughly washed the knife, and watched TV in contrite silence until the adults came home. Of course I told no one. I still, until this moment, haven't really told anyone.

To be a man as I learned it was to be contained, held within, under control. Unripped and unbroken. Everything I learned about the body early on was about control and containment. Men were not to leak or make too much noise or express too much or lose a grip on anything. Not on your body. Not on anyone else's. This makes the world a fundamentally terrifying and destabilizing place for men because what the earth is, at its spiritual core, is a thing uncontained. It is liquid and explosive, the chaos of leaves and rivers, mountains of lava, fecund and overflowing.

To be a man as manhood was taught to me is to be fiercely at odds with the earth, which is to say it is fiercely at odds with the divine. It is to be in battle with the divine because to be a man is to be in control and the divine is the complete opposite of control. This is why men are so violent and angry and destructive to ourselves and to you and to the world. We teach each other to hate what we cannot control, and nothing, literally nothing, can be truly controlled.

Look at the earth, how it insists itself upon our buildings and shopping malls and golf courses and hiking trails. Look at how we have tried for centuries to overwhelm the earth and instead the earth has overwhelmed us, calmly, innocently, and with all the tender savagery of a stream running down a gentle slope. What is a body for in the midst of that kind of simple and inevitable passing?

As boys we were trained that our bodies had one purpose, and that purpose was to deal in pain. Either you could administer pain or you could survive pain. In the body theology of the time, each of those abilities was necessary to survive the inescapable fact of when and where we were. You had to be able to receive and recover from pain because the trials and tribulations of life were such that you'd be made to hurt often. You'd have to work your ass off to make a dollar. You'd have to break your back in the mills or in the fields. You'd have to lay brick and lift heavy and put your limbs at risk.

For practice at this we played football, which meant colliding at full speed with other bodies who themselves were using immunity to pain as a form of social capital. I once saw a kid break his collarbone in a game of street football, which we, for some reason, played full contact and full tackle on cobblestone. He kept playing even though his shoulders were suddenly different heights. When we learned the next day that he had broken his collarbone, we thought he was a hero. I'm sure some part of all of us still does. We were in fourth grade.

The other point of the body was also to administer pain. You had to not only survive a broken collarbone, but you better be ready to deliver one too should the situation call for it. Giving pain was how you proved your right to exist, to be left alone, to be granted full humanity. This need was so strong that we fetishized the giving of pain. "Stick 'em!" would be the invocation whenever you delivered a particularly nasty hit on another kid. We watched TV compilations of the hardest NFL hits because we loved seeing men absolutely destroy other men: the sudden violence of it, the explosion, the cleanliness, the destruction. We wanted that power and what that power promised us. It was erotic, not yet in the sexual sense, but in the sense of a pleasure derived from the body. We watched men hitting men over and over; we sucked in our breath and felt the tingle in our spines each time.

What we did not have, as men-in-training, was access

to the body as a site of pleasure. The closest thing to that came as we grew older and the notion of sexual conquest was introduced. That brought some vague idea that we could "pleasure" a woman and that if we did so well enough, we would "win" her devotion. In that framework, pleasure was a currency, a transaction, something you traded for power. You gave pleasure; in return, you gained power.

The Everything

I had just turned eight when my mother gave me up for the second time. The first time I had been eighteen months old, and she sent me to live with her sister in McKeesport, Pennsylvania, while she went to secretary college in DC. I joined her again when I was four. We spent much of the next four years living hand to mouth. This time, she came to me on a weekday morning and asked me if I wanted to have a special day with her, which would mean skipping school and going to see *E.T.* The only thing I remember of the movie was that it was very, very sad. Or maybe it was the day that was sad. There was a heaviness. Fall was descending on us and then winter. After the movie she sat with me in the parking lot playing with the acne on her face and refusing to start the car. I could tell there was something. She said:

"How would you like to go live with your aunt and uncle in McKeesport?"

I understood, of course, that the only answer that could please her was "yes." I understood that she needed to be free of me. I understood that it was my fault we were living the way we did. I wanted to please her. I wanted her to be happy. So, I said yes. It would be another thirty-five years before I allowed myself to think that I also could have said "no."

I moved to a small steel town near Pittsburgh to live with my uncle and aunt, an interracial couple. He was responsible with a big personality and lots of jokes. She was responsible with a cold edge to her. But she could be very kind. I appreciated them taking me in. I told the kids at my new school that my parents had died in a fire, which I had narrowly escaped. As evidence, I showed everyone the birthmark on my left wrist, a vaguely heart-shaped blob where the skin was darker than it was everywhere else. This, I said, was proof that I had been burned.

It was nice to have a bedroom to sleep in and food to eat and furniture and lots and lots of orange juice, which to this day is my favorite beverage. My aunt made it in a plastic pitcher from Minute Maid frozen concentrate. I could not control myself. I drank it like it was the stuff of life. I did everything like it was the stuff of life. I came home from school, a latchkey kid, and binged cartoons while consuming container after container of yogurt, cup after cup of orange juice, bowls of ice cream, hand-fuls of cookies. I ate and drank like I was trying to sur-vive something.

A teenage babysitter molested me less than a month after I moved there. She took off her top and told me to touch her. She kissed and fondled me and told me I was cute. I missed my mother. I thought the babysitter liked me. For years, I thought the reason she did this to me was because she really liked me, and it made me feel valuable.

Their household was organized and picturesque and sometimes deeply violent. Alcoholism runs in my family. When the sun was up, my uncle was gregarious and playful, the picture of the perfect father figure. When the sun went down, he yelled and screamed, punched holes in walls, overturned furniture. I listened from my bedroom, in the dead of night, the clapboard house shaking. I made a family for myself out of stuffed ani-mals. I put them in order. Adam the Koala was my first, which is why I named him Adam, because he was the Father of Man. Then came Walter, an orangutan named for the character actor Walter Matthau. There was Buster, named after Buster Brown shoes, and Franklin, named for Benjamin Franklin, and Tito, named for Tito Jackson, the only Jackson who I thought would be okay with me borrowing his name because he was the least famous.

My aunt and uncle stressed schoolwork and respect-ability above all else. Perfection was a weapon, they told me, that I would use to survive in a world that would hate me. They checked my homework every night for years, marked every question that I got wrong and made me go back and do it again. I hated that ritual with a vitriol that I can still feel at the base of my spine today. I could not stop it. I did not have "no."

When he got really angry with my seemingly unending math errors, he would grab me by the shirt, flip me over the couch, and pounce on top of me.

Get. Your. Shit. Together, he would whisper through gritted teeth, his beard close enough for me to imagine what it would be like to one day have a beard of my own. My aunt would say his name. Quietly. Disappointedly.

You have to work twice as hard, he reminded me, *to be considered half as good.*

I did work twice as hard. I had to. There was something wrong with my brain. I had weird obsessions and tics. I had a horrible and embarrassing stutter that would crop up whenever I had to say a sentence that began with the word "I." I peed the bed until I was twelve years old. I watched the same television shows over and over, read the same books over and over until I had entire pages and scenes memorized. I sat in my room reciting TV theme songs and chapter introductions to myself. I never wanted anything new. I was terribly afraid of new things. What if the new thing rejected me? I only wanted to experience the same things on repeat because they were the only things I could trust. By the time I was in fifth grade I had gone to nine different schools and lived at countless addresses: apartments, hotels, and houses. I was afraid, so deeply afraid of everyone and everything that I developed a litany of poorly constructed defenses from the world. I cracked jokes all the time. I made it my goal to please everyone I met, to make sure that they didn't hurt me. I gave everyone what I thought they wanted. I never said no. I disappeared into obsessions and make-believe; I developed fixations, organized all sixty-four of my Matchbox cars, ranked them by coolness, held elaborate ceremonies when there was a changing of the order. I transposed the major scale into every key in my head. I counted to five thousand on Saturday afternoons. I chewed the same piece of gum for three and a half days, until it disintegrated in my mouth. I listened to music on cassette until I knew what lay within every crevice of sound, the way the clavichord could be heard for just an instant in the little gap between the bass and the guitar lick, sounding like a communication from another dimension, a dimension beneath and beyond the rest of the song, the way Michael Jackson ad-libbed "I like it" in the vamp of "Dancing Machine," his newly adult voice reedy and sensual. I obsessed over these details, I thought about them at all times, I clung to details because details made the most sense.

The other survival tool I honed was the tool of daydreaming, of never, ever tying my brain down to where I was or who I was with. This is why I made so many mistakes in my schoolwork, especially math. I was a failure at anything that required sustained attention. My mind felt like a bird whose fluttering I could control only with violence, and the violence was too brutal for me to do on myself. I hated violence of any type. I could not control my mind and I did not want to. I let it fly and dream, quivering and trembling haphazardly around the entire world of things: *Karate Kid*, Mustang Shelby, Michael Jordan, Michael Jackson, the Fat Boys, begonias, baby kangaroos, shag carpets, stenciled owls, Rudolph the Red-Nosed Reindeer, Walter Abercrombie and the draw play that the Steelers ran on first downs, Redline BMX bikes with the 360 handlebars, G.I. Joe, penises, the metallic smell of geraniums, axe murderers, Prince's Harley-Davidson, nuclear war, fat laces in checkerboard patterns, Kennywood, cobblestone, earthworms, *Benson*, *M*A*S*H*, *Three's Company*, and *WKRP* altogether, gravity, the McKeesport reservoir, the Revolutionary War, James Brown, sweet potato pie, Formica, how they made furniture curve, major and minor key transpositions, tape dubbing, NASA, wood paneling, *Donkey Kong*, basements, naked ladies, and Popsicles.

I let my aunt and uncle and teachers be the violence that trapped my mind and held it locked up. I made some of them yell at me and throw things and push me against walls and hit me with belts. I made some of them tell me that I was going to turn out just like all these other niggers dead or in jail or strung out on drugs and I didn't want to be like them, did I?

These were beautiful times for me. They do not sound like it, but they were. There was a world that kept unfolding itself with endless pleasures and distractions. I did not have to ask why niggers were on drugs. I did not have to ask where my mother was and why she didn't want me. There was no room for questions like this.

There were too many other things to think about. Even grief, even the absence of home, even the trembling clapboard of a two-story house felt like a warm cup of milk in a thick and heavy mug, laced with just the tiniest hint of sweet vanilla and whisky.

The Clothes

I missed my mother and I wanted a woman to love me. I was in seventh grade. I wore my aunt's stockings one day after school because when I looked in the mirror I saw a woman I could be safe with, who loved me and knew everything about me and still wanted to spend time with me. That woman was me. I saw little pieces of her in me all the time, but when I put on my aunt's clothes I saw her more clearly and completely, like an apparition that had come to life, like something you had dreamt about that had now appeared before you. I liked these clothes. I liked them more than my own.

I made a habit of trying them on after school. It took me three days before I got caught. My aunt and uncle handled it badly. They could not have handled it worse if they had been given a pamphlet titled *How to Handle*

Catching Your Black Preteen Adoptive Son Trying on Women's Clothing in the Worst Possible Way. They yelled. They shamed. They excommunicated. They told me it was disgusting.

I promised never to do it again. It was the first foxhole prayer of what would turn out to be many in my life. *Dear God, please keep me from ever touching the stuff again. I'll do anything. I'll be good.* God heard my prayer and relieved me. I did not touch the stuff again. I was off the juice. Three days clean by the grace of God from wearing women's clothing and liking how I looked. I had been delivered.

Unfortunately, at the end of that week my aunt found a pair of her underwear in my laundry. I had hidden them there back when I was using so I wouldn't get caught. But I forgot about them. She thought I was back on the stuff again and exploded at me. She stood in the kitchen waving them at me, yelling at me for violating her, for lying to her, for making her sick. I stood frozen in the way that I would always feel frozen when a white woman was yelling at me, accusing me of a thing I didn't do but it looked like I did.

It was all my fault. If I was normal this never would have happened. If I wasn't this way—a weirdo, a pervert, a freak, a broken boy, unmanly, unfit, abnormal—this never would have happened. Sure, in the practical sense I was being wrongly accused. But in the universal sense I was being fairly punished. God had seen that I was disgusting, and God was saying: *That's what you get.*

I mostly got over it just like I mostly got over everything. She never believed that the second pair of underwear was an accident. We did not live together much longer after that. I moved on. There was music to be discovered, and girls at school to think about, and boys at school to think about why I was thinking about, and people to fight with for calling me nigger and books to be obsessively read and reread, and reread, and reread, and reread, and reread and reread and reread like I was pinned to the bed, reread like I was trapped between the pages, reread like I was unable to move as a bug is suspended in a drop of amber for all of eternity.

But I missed the woman in the mirror. She understood me and forgave me. She was safe. It was hard to go on without her. That's life, I figured at the time. Sometimes you lose people you love—even if those people are you.

The Music

I was in the seventh grade when my aunt and uncle told me that they were getting a divorce. By then we had moved from McKeesport to a blindingly white suburb named White Oak. I got called nigger there about once a month, and I fought someone over it about twice a year. My uncle moved out. I lost contact with him. Everyone lost contact with him. These were his missing years.

When news of the divorce became final, I had to decide what to do with my life. I lived with my aunt alone for a little while longer. She loved me, but I felt like she didn't like me. I looked like my uncle. I talked like him and walked like him. She was not my blood relation.

She went to work every day, made me food, and advocated for me against racist teachers. She made me orange juice. She yelled at me. She bought me books and socks and Swatches and batteries for my Walkman, two-tone Guess jeans, and a keyboard. A Pittsburgh Steelers bedspread.

She made me feel small and ugly and broken the way she picked at everything I did wrong, the way she corrected me and seemed to be sickened by me.

She stayed up with me late into the night watching PBS science documentaries and British comedies. She posted my report cards on the refrigerator and bragged to her friends about my near-photographic memory.

She rarely hugged me.

I seemed to hurt her. She seemed hurt.

She celebrated my birthdays in increasingly sad and isolated ceremonies, baking cakes from scratch, blowing up balloons one by one.

She was an artist who worked as an attorney in family court. She was angry at men.

She drew a portrait of me sitting on my grandmother's lap from a photograph that had been taken when I was three years old. She took me to get underwear and school supplies from the department store. She made sure I had perfect attendance for three and a half years straight, and never once missed the honor roll. I did not have a lot of friends. Everyone in my neighborhood was white. Everyone in all my classes and on my school bus was white. Everyone in my home was white. I was stranded. It was like living on the moon.

My mother had since moved to Los Angeles, and around eighth grade, I had the distinct thought that there was nothing for me there in Pennsylvania so I might as well try my luck out west. I remember feeling that this was a funny thing for a child to think, but I always liked acting like a grown-up. When my classmates asked me why I was suddenly moving to California, a place no one from around there had been and that as far as anyone knew existed only on television, I told them I was going out there to become an actor. I said that so much that I started to believe it. I liked the idea that all the feelings I had might one day turn into something that I would be famous for. I liked the idea that I could get everyone to love me.

I flew to Los Angeles by myself when I was thirteen. My mother was living in a one-bedroom apartment on a tree-lined street in what is now a desirable neighborhood but then was kind of hood-adjacent. I learned to listen for helicopters every night. I made friends with the kid across the street, and we formed a skate gang called the Warriors. Our two main activities were taking the bus to Venice Beach and getting paid by the lady at the end of the block to wash her Suzuki Samurai.

We would eventually learn that she used to be famous. She had recorded a one-hit wonder in 1982 that everybody knew. She was rumored to be dating a guy from the movie *Breakin'*, which is the main reason we would do skate tricks in front of her house, hoping that he might come out to the driveway one day and just start popping and locking and we would join him and the entire thing would be like that Pepsi commercial where Michael Jackson comes out and starts dancing with an eight-year-old Alfonso Ribeiro, a.k.a. Carlton from *The Fresh Prince*. This never happened. But still I liked being around the singer a lot. She was like the first genuinely cool adult I ever knew. She had a laid-back cynicism to her that made sense to me. It was like she knew that the world was trash, nothing was that interesting to her, but still kids should be treated with kindness, you should still dress with some flair, and it was important to tend to your rosebushes. She made me feel like I was normal because that was exactly how I felt.

At the beginning, the best thing about being in LA was being around Black people again. For the first year or so mostly everyone I knew was Black. My second cousins lived downstairs in the same apartment building, my friends across the street and next door were Black, my entire school bus was Black. Our bus driver was Black and bore more than a passing resemblance to Kool Moe Dee, which he played up by always wearing fake Porsche Carrera wraparounds. *What up, Kool Moe*, we would say when we got on the bus. *Yeah, yeah*, he would reply. He used to play KDAY on the bus, at the time an AM radio station and the only rap station in Los Angeles. In Pennsylvania I had been limited mostly to rap that had already crossed over to white kids like the Beastie Boys, Run-DMC, and Fresh Prince. Here in LA, I had access to better, deeper Golden Era stuff.

Of particular interest to me were EPMD and Rakim, whose videos I used to watch at the house of a girl in my neighborhood. She was my age and went to the same school I did. Her family had just moved to LA from the Bay Area and she was always putting us up on the latest Bay culture. We heard messy MC Hammer bootlegs from live parties and watched videos of him that looked like they were shot on someone's home video camera. We crowded around to watch dilapidated VHS recordings of Too $hort, Oaktown's 357, Troop. She was my first kiss, my first make-out. She showed me how to eat her out. We would practice after school until she patted me on the head and told me I was doing it right. We rewound the video for Biz Markie's "Vapors" so many times that the tape broke.

Big Daddy Kane, Rodney-O and Joe Cooley, King T, De La Soul, Rob Base and DJ E-Z Rock, Public Enemy, Redhead Kingpin, Jungle Brothers, Stetsasonic, BDP, Ultramagnetic, Ice-T, Tone-Loc, Marley Marl, MC Lyte, Kid 'n Play, Audio Two, LA Dream Team, Steady B, X-Clan, Sir Mix-a-Lot, J. J. Fad, Three Times Dope, 2 Live Crew, Heavy D, Kool G Rap and DJ Polo, Busy Bee, Nice & Smooth, Special Ed, Gang Starr, Kwamé the Boy Genius, Chubb Rock. A pantheon. An array of gods. Asymmetrical haircuts, undercuts with three or four perfectly lined parts on the short side, glittering medallions, custom-made leather tracksuits with crispy clean sneakers. Everything Black people made was so beautiful, so absolutely impeccable. I found us gorgeous. Every day someone tries to teach me that we are ugly. Every day I have to remember that we are not. This is why I spend so much time with my eyes closed and my face dappled by the afternoon sun. I am remembering that we are beautiful.

I loved her, this girl from up north. I don't know how seriously she took me. It didn't matter. She had already had a hard life, it seemed. She talked about murders and violence where she came from. She told the stories like they were funny. But she was a kid. We were all kids. I was intimidated a little bit by her, and my ego and intense feeling that I was "less than" sometimes stressed me out when I was around her. But mostly I just liked it when she seemed happy. I was never her boyfriend; she always had a real boyfriend, someone who was cooler than me, older than me. Somebody with a six-pack and Jordans and a car and a Jheri curl and sometimes a gun. I was goofy. A square. A buster. I didn't mind, even though I was vaguely aware that I should have minded.

When we lay on the couch after school watching videos and eating corn nuts that we shoplifted from the liquor store next to the laundromat, that was when I felt most at home, most loved. Boys then and boys today will tell you that this is being a simp. That is because boys work very hard to keep each other from truly valuing another person's feelings. I don't know why we do this, but we do. But the thing is, I was happy. I was with someone I liked, watching videos I loved, eating liberated snacks, and occasionally tasting the warm soft metal of her flesh while she sighed above me. What problem with this could I possibly have? I once interviewed a rancher for a piece in a music magazine about cowboy poetry and I asked him what made people happy, in his opinion. He said:

*The key to happiness, I think, is to be a part of a commu-
nity, and to make something of value for that community.*
She was my community; my kisses were something of
value for her. Therefore, I was happy.

We were evicted again. Eviction was the one thing
you could always count on. If you had something, it
would be lost. If you lived somewhere, you would have to
move. These were the rules. I stayed briefly with the pas-
tor of a church that I was sporadically attending while
my mother finessed her way into another roommate situation in Inglewood. After a few weeks I joined her. I knew
that this was the beginning of another round of chaos. I
didn't pay too much attention to it this time. I had learned
it was better that way.

I decided to take the actor thing seriously. I had started
auditioning for school plays and I got the lead in three
consecutive shows in ninth grade. I was bussed to a
school in Brentwood, a wealthy LA neighborhood where
O. J. Simpson lived around the corner. We'd sometimes
see him taking a walk or grabbing a meal at the restaurant at the bottom of the hill. It was before. The school
had the whole world on its campus, and I liked it. Hood
kids, Black middle-class kids, kids who could dunk in
the ninth grade, gangbangers, average white kids, white
kids whose parents were in the industry (producers and
agents) or whose R-rated seventies comedies me and my
half brother used to sneak and watch after the grown-
ups went to sleep, surfers, stoners, baby goths, Persian
kids with several different kinds of jewelry, girls named
Brooke who had high ponytails and scrunchies and wore

Birkenstocks with socks and shorts, kids who were never in school because they always had some legal case or other and who, when they were in school, pressed me for wearing a red sweatshirt and made me take it off even though I was wearing nothing underneath and had to go to the office to get an ill-fitting Ocean Pacific shirt from lost and found. LA was pretty and incongruous and absurd and absolutely endless, an entire world presented in vast miniature, endlessly curving around palm trees and cop cars like a dirty mandala. It made a perfect kind of sense to me.

Everyone started knowing me as the guy in all the plays, and I felt like I had an identity. I was that actor kid. It became important to me to keep all the chaos of my homelife hidden away. I spent much of the year sick with malnutrition, but I didn't want anyone to know. I went to school with flus and colds so bad that I remember sitting in history class shivering and sweating and occasionally hallucinating. They called my mother from work and the police searched my locker because they thought I was on drugs. I developed a stomach issue that bothered me all year. I once told my gym teacher that I couldn't do the daily six-hundred-meter run because I was feeling sick, and I might throw up. He did not believe me, I assumed at the time because he thought Black kids were full of shit, so he said, "Well throw up while you run," and I did. I ran the length of the track puking and pushing myself, puking and pushing myself. It was nice to prove him wrong but the part I loved most was proving to myself that I could push past anything. That was important to me, to feel like there was no force in this world that I couldn't outlast if I just applied enough will to it. I needed to feel like I was untouchable. That made me feel safe. I did not ever want to be touched.

I won a $500 citywide acting competition. I took the bus there alone for preliminaries, semifinals, and finals. I gave my mother the check and we used it to buy groceries. It made me feel like a man. She was proud of me. She almost cried. A Beverly Hills agent who was in the audience signed me and sent me on auditions where I was always reading for the part of Crackhead Informant #1 and Ghetto Street Youth #3. I never got a part. I went to an arts high school to study acting and decided that I was most definitely going to win an Oscar. I was possibly the most talented actor in the world as far as I could tell. It was Denzel and then me, basically. We started doing Shakespeare, which I loved. His words were music and he had written about every single feeling a human being could have. Teachers would sit with us in small groups and go over the entire text of *The Winter's Tale* or *A Midsummer Night's Dream* line by line by line. It would take a semester to get through one play, learning what every word meant, how every caesura between a word that ends with an *s* and another that begins with one should be delivered. We examined his use of consonants and vowels, of *k*'s and *p*'s and *f*'s, *Gallop apace, you fiery-footed steeds . . . O for a muse of fire that would ascend / The brightest heaven of invention . . . Thy mother plays, and I / Play too, but so disgraced a part, whose issue / Will hiss me to my grave, contempt and clamor / Will be my knell . . .* My compulsive brain would latch on to these lines and I would not be able to shake them loose. They played over and over in my head. I broke them down, thought about why they were written in the exact way they were. I did that with all text. *Crowd rockin' mutha-fucka from around the way, / I got a six-shooter, yo mean hombre . . . The words from our direction, the gold boy section / Kicking like Bruce Lee's* Chinese Connection . . . *I take my time just before I manifest a rhyme, / Sharp and accurate can stop the music on a dime . . . I'm the epitome born to get lyrical, / For you to beat me it's gonna take a miracle.* I let text caress me and sing me to sleep.

We spent the next few years moving around, first to Inglewood, where I listened to Mustang 5.0s vibrating the concrete with bass that Mos Def would later say was an ancient mating call, then Van Nuys, where I wandered wide boulevards with Fishbone and Sonic Youth in my ears and the relentless Valley sun beating down on me, wearing a cutoff black Ocean Pacific T-shirt and Chuck Taylors with Jimi Hendrix lyrics written on them in the Sharpie I shoplifted to begin my career as a tagger. I tagged Zeus on bus benches and in Taco Bell bathrooms because I wanted everyone taking a shit to feel like the god of gods was always present. That is still why I write.

I had a gun pointed at me by some gangbangers who were riding around playing Halloween pranks on kids. They hopped out of the car and chased me and when they found me cowering in the entrance to a library they laughed and said, *Ah, we was just fucking with you, fool*, but they didn't put the gun away.

We lived in the dark because my mother couldn't pay the electric bill. I did homework by candlelight and went downstairs to the car to see what time it was. We didn't have a phone. I climbed the fence to the elementary school behind the parking lot to use the pay phone there, where I ran up a $500 bill on the calling card number my friend Hannah's parents shared with me because they felt bad for me.

I spent summer days at home, hungry, watching *Gilligan's Island* and Spike Lee movies over and over again, and I learned that I could survive on two dollars' worth of food a day if I went to the Korean liquor store to buy a gallon of water and a pack of cookies and ate it all very, very slowly.

That was the key, you see. You had to pay attention to everything. Every bite, every sip, every moment of fatigue and hope on the blazing and smoggy concrete and stucco. It might be all you would ever have. You had to know how to make it last.

The Police

My mother got arrested for writing a bad check to buy a mattress and they took her to jail one morning before school. I came out of the shower in our stucco apartment wearing only a towel and found myself face-to-face with two plainclothes LAPD officers. We never had anyone in our home and these men were big, it seemed. They towered over our whole life. My mother was in handcuffs. My nakedness terrified me. I had watched them beat Rodney King on television not even a month prior. As far as my body knew, these were the same men who did that. As far as I knew, Rodney King's sweat and blood were still in the fabric of their clothing. They searched my underwear drawer for contraband. One white dude, one mixed dude. I recognized them from a few weeks earlier when they had been coming out of the apartment complex, presumably having just missed the chance to execute the warrant, when we walked in. My mother, a legendary flirt, had smiled broadly, batted her eyelashes, and made a joke to me about how they were hot. I rolled my eyes. She was always flirting. I acted like I hated it, but secretly I thought it was nice that it made her happy to be pretty.

Now I stood there, small and quiet and wet on a Thursday morning at 8:00 a.m. while they restrained her wrists in front of me. She asked one of them, the light-skinned dude, to fetch a twenty-dollar bill from her purse and give it to me, which he did with the solemnity of someone bestowing a knighthood. She told me that she didn't know when she'd be back. The Black cop asked me if I was going to be alright. I knew what the answer to this was supposed to be. It was not a question, but a pronouncement of a job. "You gonna be alright, man?" The "man" at the end to make sure that I remembered who I was.

Yeah, I'll be fine.

I was fine. Just alone. The silence of that apartment that morning after they strutted off with my mother in handcuffs, that is the silence of my writing desk at this moment. A weighted silence, a silence pregnant with tears, ready to burst as rain clouds before a summer storm.

I went to school in a carefully chosen outfit. My favorite jeans. A Mickey Mouse turtleneck that I bought off my half brother with money I had made sweeping up hair in the salon my mother went to. It felt like the first outfit of my adulthood. Light, playful references to hip-hop culture (for whatever reason Mickey Mouse was hot in the hood that year) but with my own spin on it. I faced the nights feeling lonely. I faced the days feeling free. I was on my own. I knew how to survive. It was my superpower.

Maybe that, too, is one of the days I learned about the ending of things. I would say it was the ending of my childhood but I hate clichés even when I use them. I hate knowing that what happened to me is just the thing that happens to thousands, millions of us here. We are separated from our homes and safety and our parents, left with a twenty-dollar bill that we have to make stretch for an unknown period of time, facing daytime talk shows, wide boulevards with never-ending traffic, an unrelenting sun reflecting off stucco and concrete, another TV show and another one and another one, each half-hour one a small step downward.

I lived alone until she came back a few days later. It was a small eternity, probably because it is still happening. Just as the snow did not care, the sun did not care either. Even though it was beautiful and warm and we sang songs to praise it.

I watched Rodney King get beat on television over and over again. I thought it didn't faze me, but I started locking my bedroom door for no reason. I watched a Korean liquor store owner shoot a fifteen-year-old girl in the back of the head. I watched it over and over. I thought it didn't faze me but my stutter got worse. The only time I could be sure it wouldn't happen was when I was onstage.

I came home from rehearsals of the summer production of *Carnival* to find that we were evicted again. My mother told me I'd have to find a place to live. I went to rehearsal the next day and made up a story about being kicked out for being gay. The female lead, an opera singer whose own life was falling apart, let me sleep in her living room in Tarzana. It was a weird three months. I told her I was in love with her. She told me she was flattered but she could not return my affections because I was a child. She was like thirty-five.

I tagged along with her on errands to the bank and the dry cleaners while we listened to R.E.M. together in her slightly busted-up golden Camaro. She told me about her shitty marriage to a cellist who reminded me of the bad rich boyfriend from eighties movies. We avoided him together by driving around the valley and listening to the song "Shiny Happy People" all the time. Rewinding, rewinding, rewinding, rewinding. The jangling of the guitar and the harmonies, the pop perfection of the bass climbing and falling, the relentless backbeat, that audacity to be aggressively devoid of any hint of syncopation, the whitest shit ever, quarter notes like robots, steady and unseasoned, the way the first F-sharp minor chord of the verse opens up a hole in the bottom of the song that you just keep falling through every time they play it, the way Michael Stipe's voice always sounds flat and doleful like someone contemplating suicide at a house party even though it is a perfectly fine party. Like no offense to the party but I might have to hang myself. I wanted to make people feel the way that song made me feel. Because I had that feeling and I didn't want to have it alone.

The Finger

Standing with my skateboard in the parking lot of a 7-Eleven in Van Nuys I had a sudden memory of a television show I had obsessed over when I was a kid. It was a detective action comedy called *Sonny Spoon*. Mario Van Peebles was a low-rent private eye in eighties Los Angeles who lived in a huge downtown loft with the mattress on the floor and plenty of sunlight. He was impossibly handsome, charming, and smart. He never had any money, though, and he was always conning people. There weren't that many action shows with Black protagonists, so I was transfixed. I wanted to be just like him, running around LA, romancing women, looking good shirtless, getting shot at, solving crimes using my vast networks of street informants, dressing up in funny costumes to infiltrate the bad guys and gain intel.

In one scene Spoon needed some information from a newspaper to solve a case. Rather than spending the money to buy one, he pulled this cool maneuver where he posted up next to a newspaper box and leaned casually against a wall. It was the kind of newspaper box where you put a quarter in and it unlocks the door. You then lift the door, grab your paper, and let the door drop. Spoon waited for some white guy to put a quarter in, then, when the guy walked away, he quickly grabbed the door before it slammed shut, got the paper, found the clue, solved the case.

I was about fifteen when I thought to try this at the 7-Eleven. I, too, waited coolly with my foot up on the wall. Soon enough a white guy came to buy a paper. When he let go of the door and it began to slam shut I quickly reached in to grab a paper, Spoon-style. I guess I mistimed it or forgot to grab the handle or something because while my hand was in the box the guy tried to slam it shut. He didn't want me to have a free paper.

I got most of my hand out, but my finger remained inside the box, trapped between the metal edges of the door. He kept pushing. I didn't care about the paper anymore. I just wanted my finger out. Neither of us spoke. We looked into each other's eyes while he pushed with all his weight on my finger, which was now being crushed between the two sharp metal edges of the door and the box. It was a sunny day. I looked for something in his eyes, pity, remorse . . . Maybe if he saw me, saw that I was a child, he would let me go. He did not. I saw a shaking in his eyes, desperate, trembling fear, his face red, his veins popping, his blond mustache vibrating with effort.

I finally pulled my hand from where it was trapped but not before the flesh was ripped off by the metal, exposing white meat on my middle finger, at first pale and throbbing, then quickly covered in blood, which rose from within my finger like water being squeezed from a dish sponge. A large flag of skin dangled from the bottom of the nail, translucent in the afternoon light.

We both stood in silence for a moment. Then the man quickly made for his car.

"Do you see what you did?" I yelled, waving my finger at him. It was all I could think to say. It felt risky. Confrontational. I normally would not have said anything. I did not like confronting people. But I was shaking.

He looked at me once more from inside his car, his face flushed, before he backed up and sped out of the parking lot into traffic.

This was my fault, I reasoned at the time, for wanting to be like a cool detective. What a childish thing to do, playacting stuff I'd seen on a TV show that got canceled after fifteen episodes.

On that day I saw for the first time that there are those who would rather see flesh ripped from a Black child's body than to see that Black child get away with stealing a newspaper. I looked directly into his eyes. I know what a person like that looks like up close. I know what it's like when they breathe on you, when they are sweating inches from you, when they are pushing with all their might on you.

It's a small thing. My finger healed. I'm not even sure, now, which hand it was.

But also, a thing like that, it goes on forever. It is almost everything. Not everything, but almost.

Sometimes I think if you've never had a white man look at you the way I was looked at that day, then with all due resepct, you may not understand anything, anything at all, about what any of this really is.

The Police Again

The second time someone pointed a loaded gun at my face I was seventeen.

I mean it was my fault because I was in the wrong place at the wrong time. That wrong place was in the alley behind my apartment building in Los Angeles, California, and that wrong time was April 29, 1992, at 4:48 in the afternoon. That was day one of the Los Angeles Riots.

Someone in another building called the police on me because I had gone out there to sneak a cigarette and I looked to them like a person who might burn down the building and loot the apartment, which is to say I looked Black. When two LAPD cars came screaming up to me, I didn't know what was happening. Their guns were in my face before I could truly comprehend what it meant to once again have guns in my face.

There is a funny thing that happens at the beginning of an exchange like that, a moment when you know that someone has decided that they might kill you if they feel like it, and it has literally nothing to do with who you actually are or what you are doing, but instead with what they have decided you are, with what they have been telling themselves for centuries that you are.

The funny thing is that your body breaks situations into manageable parts and handles it in shifts.

The part of your body that is worried about being permanently destroyed, blown wide open and then shredded into tatters like cloth by tiny lead projectiles that can be released from their aluminum alloy chambers with a mere five pounds of pressure from a stranger's finger takes a back seat. It graciously hands the controls over to the part of your body that is concerned with more prosaic and immediate things, like what to do with the lighter you are holding when you put your hands up, and how to effectively and safely lie down on the concrete as directed without using your hands at all.

Meanwhile, another part of your body is remembering that your mother is inside the tiny Studio City apartment you share, not twenty feet from where you now stand, and that she is terrified in general because this is already a day of great terror and anger. She is a thirty-eight-year-old Black woman in America, which means she has had great terror and anger buried in her body to begin with and has had it since she was about twenty weeks into gestation in *her* mother's womb, which is the time by which you began in the form of her eggs. But also, maybe it goes back to when *her* mother was at twenty weeks' gestation in *her* mother's womb, which is when she had My-Mother-the-Egg in *her* body, and maybe it goes back even further than that. Maybe we carry the feelings of our mothers' bodies all the way back to the beginning of our mothers.

The part of your body that remembers that your mother is inside the apartment also remembers that she is connected to you—tethered, you might say, in very much the same way that scientists now believe that particles of light remain tethered across the vastness of space (they call this quantum entanglement, which is one of the better phrases I've heard in the past few years).

That part of your body remembers to move very quietly and to make the exchange with the officers very chill so that she doesn't have reason to come outside and be confronted with the image of men holding guns on her baby, the very baby she carried in her womb and then in her arms for all those precious years.

The part of your body that remembers that your mother is inside the apartment is also the part that suddenly and inexplicably in that moment remembers what it felt like to be held by her in her arms, close to her chest, the warmth of her breath bathing you much in the way the towering redwoods bathe the streams and the rocks and mycelium that run and grow beneath them. That part of your body also remembers that no one has held you in years. Not your mother, not anyone. You have only held yourself. You have only started growing hair in weird places and smelling badly and picking at zits on the tip of your nose so obsessively that they explode into a fountain of pus that you need to hide with toilet paper in second-period history class.

That part of your body suddenly remembers what it's like to be held by her and the way it felt was like home, yes, but also it was like more than home, it was like oneness, like the simplest answer to the most complicated, unanswerable questions. And that part also knows that if it felt that way for you, then it must have felt doubly, tri-ply, no, *infinitely* more meaningful and overwhelming for her to be holding you as it did for you to be held by her. And that part of you wants nothing less than for her to see your life now, in this moment held not by her but in the hands of men who do not know who you are, know only what they have decided for centuries that you are. So the part of your body that remembers what it was like to be held by your mother takes pains to move slowly, carefully, quietly, respectfully, with the gentleness of a child cradling a ladybug on a scented geranium petal, so as not to cause an undue ruckus or create unnecessary emotions while there are loaded guns pointed at your face. Your body learns how to never, ever create undue ruckus or unnecessary emotions while there are guns pointed at your face, and your body learns that there are always guns pointed at your face.

And finally, there's a part of your body that quietly reminds you that everything is alright, that it's all going to be fine and that even if you die right here, which you absolutely might, death is but a moment, a blip on the never-ending cosmic waves that we forever ride, that you are tethered to your ancestors just as particles of light are tethered across space-time. And in that moment your body allows you to feel the presence of all reality and all of humanity, right there in your solar plexus. And you can even see beyond humanity to a place where everything happens in slow motion and it becomes possible to see— no, to *feel, to exist*—through all of time and space and generations, and to suddenly have a window into all the stars that ever were and to feel them in your body. And that feeling is the feeling of absolute nothingness. And that nothingness is terrifying in its utter lack of terror, its utter emotional and spiritual silence. Never in your life has anything been so devoid of terror. Never in your life has anything been so still, so deprived of existence. You are in the space between life and chaos and you know that you have been there before, and that you are always there. Even when, as you will have to do in a few moments, you come back. To here. Where everyone else is.

And so you just drop your cigarette to the concrete real smooth and put up your hands and crack a joke or two and tell them, when they ask, that you go to an arts high school and they seem impressed by this, so you make small talk about the acting business with them until they put their guns away and tell you to be more careful next time. And you thank them and shake their hands and agree that you should be more careful next time, and you go inside to where your mother is waiting.

And you and your mother watch the news together for days in silence, the burning at Florence and Normandie, the snipers near Baldwin Hills Crenshaw Plaza, where you had gotten your ear pierced and your first pair of cross cords, which felt like a very big deal at the time. You watch the smashing of windows, people making off with television sets and home appliances, and you keep thinking about the sniper who was picking off cops from a rooftop and you start to realize that there is a place right between life and death, where if you got stuck there, it is entirely possible to kill another person.

And most of all, you never, *ever* tell your mother what happened because you don't want her to know about the cigarettes. So instead, you watch the news together in silence, where you are seeing a whole city burned into the sky and she shakes her head and says: "It's a goddamn shame." And you say nothing.

And every night for the next week or so you wake up with the feeling that there is a tiger in your room, inches from your bed, and though you can't see it, you can *feel* it. It is big and violent and smelly and still and very angry, and your body reacts as though the tiger is there.

Your pupils widen, your mouth dries, your stomach tightens. Your muscles wind themselves up, ready to spring. You awaken like this in the middle of the night, and your brain can't figure out why, since there's really nothing happening, but your body knows.

It knew then and knows now, and it has not forgotten.

It won't ever forget, no matter how much or how desperately you want it to. It won't forget. Your body knew how to keep you alive in the moment when you were almost killed. And your body won't ever, no matter how much you beg it to, let that moment go.

The Smoke

Once I found drugs and alcohol it was hard to tell which came first, the depression or the depressives, but everything synced up and I felt like I was a complete person because I was both the destroyer and the destroyed.

Drugs are like a very quick and easy way to overwrite your reality, kind of like an Instagram takeover but for your consciousness, and when you are high you can post whatever you want, and it doesn't matter because it wasn't you making the decisions. And the first time I was high I was seventeen and I kept thinking, *This is it! This is the life!* and I could not get enough of that feeling, and I kept wondering where I could get more of it, so when I went to college and the kids sent me to buy a six-pack of Corona on the first weekend because I was the only one with something of a mustache, I also bought a forty-ounce of Crazy Horse for myself and hid it under my bed and took sips while everyone else was struggling with their Coronas.

And I started hiding vodka in water bottles before my first week of college was out and drinking in secret and falling in love with the feeling that no one knew everything there was to me. These fools. I was pretending to be a regular kid in the dorms with all the regular kids, putting posters on walls, watching *The Kids in the Hall*, jamming out on guitar, saying "dude" and "bro" all the time, but I had a secret that they could never understand, and I wanted it that way because that way was the only way that felt right. The secret was that I was slowly rotting from the inside; the secret was that I knew what it was like to have a loaded gun pointed at me; the secret was that I knew what it was like to not eat for thirty-three hours, which up until that point was my record; the secret was that I knew what it was like to see through time, to see everything there has ever been because you were stuck between life and death, and I didn't want anyone around me to know that secret because it was mine, it was what made me who I was, and I knew that they would take that if they could, and so I sealed the secret in, spackled it shut inside me with weed, acid, red wine, white wine, Pacifico, mushrooms, and whatever else I could get my hands on.

I went to a theater conservatory in New York. It was a studio where we could learn how to make weird downtown performance art if we wanted to, and I wanted to. I spent three days a week in the studio from nine to five rolling on the floor, breaking down texts, doing contact improv and scene work, choreographing dances, being around other kids who were not like me entirely, most of them were rich suburban kids who were going to be cosplaying as edgy artists for a while before buying a house near a creek in a neighborhood that I would be reluctant to walk through. But there was also the occasional weird isolated kid like me, the kid who had moved around and slept on kitchen floors and was making art with a violence that they needed to match the violence they felt inside of them, and I did love those kids even if I didn't know them well because it's hard for hurt teenagers to know anyone well.

I went to school, made theater all the time, barely did any other schoolwork, took every job I could find. Bike messenger, telephone fundraiser, actor in Germany, actor in New York, pasta delivery boy, barista, waiter. I did it all while high and drunk and I made being high and drunk while doing normal things into a superpower. If I was high and drunk and no one knew it, then that meant no one was really seeing me. And I made not being seen into a superpower. I tried to date but I was a terrible person to date, I suspect. I was fighting with myself all the time. Trying to be loving and caring on the one hand and hating everyone who was kind to me on the other. I was like most addicts. I was like my uncle. I was sweet, and charismatic, and responsible, and good-natured. I was like my uncle: cruel, and selfish, and resentful, and deeply frightened.

I graduated from college and tried my hand at marriage. I met Lee because she was dating a guy who I was directing in a play who was cheating on her with my roommate who I was also fooling around with, and also Lee was the roommate of someone I worked at a café with who I was also fooling around with. Lee pursued me, which I liked. She showed up to my performances and brought me carrot juice and left rambling, awkward messages on voice mail, which all my roommates heard and teased me about. We went on a date on October 17, 1997, and by the time we sat on the banks of the East River, and we had run out of things to talk about, and she looked at me like, *So are you gonna kiss me now or what*, I knew that I was going to marry her for real and that we would have two kids together. I just knew it the same way I knew that my mother would be killed if she came out of the house that Wednesday afternoon during the LA Riots. I knew it because sometimes you just know in some invisible place that you carry around with you but that isn't even you when things are ending and new things are being born.

I knew it because in that kiss I felt the sudden disappearance of all questions. I had a life that was overrun with questions. *Do I exist? Am I good enough? Am I a human? Who is going to kill me? Will I be destroyed? Do I matter?* I stayed drunk and high because I found that if I could get just the right buzz going, those questions would disappear and I would feel, for a brief moment, like a human being rather than a rat king of fears and insecurities. I had not yet accepted that feeling like a rat king of insecurities was part of being a human being.

The freedom would last for only a moment before the panic and regret and paranoia would take over, but that moment was glorious enough that I was willing to do almost anything to feel it again. Just one more time. When I kissed Lee, I felt that moment. I felt it completely sober. I felt another person feeling that moment. I knew that I would give up anything for it. I tried to. I had to. I don't know. I thought it might be the only way I could survive.

The Birth

We had two kids; they were both born at home.
My son came first in March 2003. I caught him in my
two hands, and in the instant before he cried, he gave me
a look that I will never forget. Like he was surprised to be
here, like a doll that had just come to life and had no idea
why. It was absurd and frightening and enchanting and
miraculous all at once. There was a soul. It was inside the
tiniest of little bodies with tiny little fingers and toes and
swirls of black hair, and that soul had come here from
where I did not know, and its first act on this planet was
to look directly at me and wail. If someone can bring you
to life by simply looking at you, then that is what this
person did to me.

Our daughter was born two and a half years later and
I caught her whole body, which was huge and magnificent,

just before she landed on our bed, and she cried right away, pink and filled to the absolute brim with oxygen and air and the wind from the giant bird of prey that perched outside our home, looking at us and ruffling her enormous wings the entire time she was being born.

We held her and kissed her and touched her perfect little hairs on her head and my son listened to her mewing and observed, "*She sounds like a sheep!*" and we all laughed. It was our first family laugh of our newly complete family, a family that would go on to spend hundreds perhaps thousands of hours laughing hysterically at anything and everything. And I felt like a true human being for those months, caring for Lee, performing moxibustion at her feet so that the baby would turn around in utero (*it worked!!*), cooking the placenta into a weird wine cocktail we had read about online (*it also worked!!*), and feeding Lee Floradix after the baby came.

I watched Lee go to the other side of reality to birth these people. Her head reared back on the couch, the afternoon sky took over her face, the midwife and doula created a gravitational field around our home. They held my hand and said every single word like an incantation. I had never seen any human beings do anything more authoritative, more potent, more magnificent than I saw the three of them—Lee and the midwife and the baby—do together. It made the rest of the world as I understood it feel like it had been made of cardboard the whole time and I was just now finding out about it. It changed my understanding of all life. It started to break me open, it evolved how I understood what my job was on this earth. Not right away, but slowly, steadily over time. My job was life. It was to enable life, to support life, to make room for life, to hold life. It was to push away everything that challenged life, that neglected life, that worked against life. My job would have to be babies and love and homes and families and safety. I wish that I could have changed into a different person in that instant, but that is not how change works.

Change instead is recovery. Change is slow and painful and confusing and uncomfortable and unclear. Change is death and life, a tearing away of everything that needs tearing away for life to grow, a leaf breaking through the stem, wrenching away the fibers of the plant's flesh, a sometimes-violent ripping of the skin, a rupture of the cocoon, a severing of everything that holds you bound up with your weakness, your harm, your shitty behavior, your abuse. Change is god, giving and taking life in patterns that do not make sense but are happening with a force that you simply cannot deny just as you cannot deny the coming and going of the waves at the edge of the land, the rushing of water, the unremitting sheets of rain.

I had to change because I was living too small, I was hurting too much, I was hurting too many other people. But I did not know how to change. I only started to get tiny sensations like pinpricks of light from stars and glitter all over my skin in the darkness and silence of faded and interminable nights. I only started to get the feeling that change for me would have to begin with some kind of surrender, some kind of softness, some kind of loosening of my grip; on what I did not know, on whom I could not say.

At moments it would begin with the feeling, very loosely, very sporadically, that it was no longer necessary for me to be filled with anything. It was not necessary for me to hold everything inside me, cementing it shut with drugs and isolation; that actually what the world needed of me, this violent, hateful world, this world that would see my blood run in the asphalt gutters, this world that would take these women and break them in two, consume them, ruin them, and then blame them for their ruination, this world that would watch us starve, and die in the snow, this world needed me to become something empty, something to be filled with god, something to be filled with love, whatever that was.

The End

Anyway, you can't do a marriage that well when you are drinking and depressed, it turns out. One afternoon, soon after we got married but before we had kids and when I was about twenty-seven years old, it dawned on me that things would be better if I were dead. Not like in any dramatic way but just in a normal way, like: *Wow, I'm not sure I'm up to this job at the youth nonprofit I work at; come to think of it, I'm not really up to any task. I'm kind of a loser and you know what would actually make things work out a lot better for everyone is if I were dead.*

This was before the kids. After the kids, I still felt this way, but I couldn't actually die over it because there were kids and they seemed to always need food and hugs and story time and playdates, and diaper changes and bikes assembled, and boo-boos kissed, and dad jokes told, and milk warmed up and vomit cleaned off their clothes. It is hard to find time and space to surrender to your own death under these circumstances. Additionally, I felt that my mother really did not deserve to outlive her only child. What kind of a thing is that for a woman to have to experience, not to mention Lee, who certainly did not need to spend the rest of her life dealing with the fact that some dude she married killed himself right after the wedding, which would certainly fuck a person up.

No, even though I wanted to die, I couldn't figure out how to do it without bumming everyone else out, so I channeled all my death instincts into a long, slow, very casual form of self-destruction that I foolishly thought would impact only me. I drank and smoked and drugged and ate whatever I wanted even when I hated it, and stayed up all night with cigarettes swearing that in the morning I would get my life together, but I never could. I did not want my life together. I wanted someone else's life and I didn't even want that, really. I did not want to exist if I didn't have to. Nevertheless the days came and went.

Lee had her own demons and we tried and tried to make our love the most important thing between us and at times it was. It is wonderful to grow up with someone the way we grew up together, burying parents together, having children together, crying on couches, laughing maniacally at precisely how stupid and hilarious and wonderfully foolish literally every human endeavor was, including our own, sitting on the floor at the end of the day, our feet in each other's laps, unpacking everything we had been holding. We marveled over the love of our children together, the infinities behind their eyes, the way they seemed to grow without any help from us, their little fingers clinging to wooden toys or melting Popsicles or fleshy earlobes, just the same way that any of us cling to life.

But we drank and drank, and when you drink like this—addictively, compulsively, without your control or even your consent—it doesn't matter in the end what you believe. The alcohol becomes what you believe. It becomes your life, your partner, your religion, your family.

First you start figuring out how to work your drinking around your family. Then you start figuring out how to work your family around your drinking. You cannot express or even hear or even feel or even understand the true call of love. Love remains an idea, a set of feelings, a theme song to a TV show that you haven't watched in decades but have the fondest memories of. You know it is there, you know it has touched you, but you cannot hear it over the relentless sloshing and spinning of active addiction. You keep reaching for it, and sometimes you will swear up and down that you have it, but it is like a fire alarm screaming and screaming for you in the real world and you are like someone trapped in the heaving, undulating currents of an ever-deepening dream. Just five more minutes.

The Death

My mother died in my arms just as I was born into hers. She had lung cancer. I knew she would go that way because she smoked a pack a day every day since about 1971. When I got the news that she had tumors in her lungs and brain, the house in Maryland that she had bought with a subprime mortgage had been foreclosed upon. It was 2007. She didn't know she had been foreclosed upon. I left Lee and the kids in California and moved to Maryland to live with her and help. It put terrible strain on my marriage. It never recovered.

My mother had two boxes of unopened mail and no furniture. A mattress, a television. Just like when I was a kid. But I was thirty-four. I pored over the envelopes. Bank notices, notices of foreclosure. Notices of sale, notices of eviction. She asked me to call the bank and beg for another chance. I did it on her behalf even though I knew it was pointless. She had not started chemo yet but still she was throwing up and having diarrhea over her mattress. I cleaned it up as best I could while I waited on hold for the bank. When I finally got someone on the phone my mother had fallen asleep. QVC was on in the background.

The bank said that the house had already been repossessed and sold and that they were sending sheriffs to evict us. A few days later they came. It was close to Christmas. Fortunately, by then my mother was in the hospital again, so she didn't have to face them. I went to her home by myself, took the bright pink notice from the door, and packed everything she still had left in her life. It was not much, really. Most of it had been lost, sold, repossessed, left behind again and again and again over the past thirty years. She was starting over when she was dying. She was always starting over.

When I was fifteen, I was trying to become a man, not so much by choice as by social and cultural momentum. Becoming a man meant that I had to be responsible. In America the first way I knew to be responsible was capitalism, since making money was the same as "handling your business," which is what men do. So, I made it my mission to constantly disapprove of my mother. This is entry-level stuff. To be a man, a certain percentage of your feeling toward women must be disapproval. You must view them as too emotional, too loud, not rational enough, unpredictable, disorganized, silly, curved, loose, untrustworthy, wrong, too much, or too little. Too forward, or too timid. It doesn't so much matter what it is that they are doing, so long as you know that they are doing it incorrectly.

I disapproved of the fact that we weren't eating, that our home wasn't safe from eviction. I disapproved of the fact that our car was repossessed a week before I turned sixteen. I disapproved of the fact that she still shopped, bought clothes, sang songs, laughed at the TV, seemed to be trying to have joy without having money. I disapproved of the ways her life left me feeling isolated, alone. I disapproved of the fact that the morning she was arrested for a bad check was the beginning and end of an entire life for me. She came back a few days later, but it was clear by then that we had both changed.

She told me the stories of her incarceration as stand-up material. The beefy lesbian at Sybil Brand, how she was just an innocent pretty woman among all these hood chicks. She was performing a bit that she frequently performed—the "I'm too beautiful to be here" shtick. It was rarely serious, mostly a joke on her preciousness, her youngest-child vibes and Cancer sensitivity. I played along by rolling my eyes. I was the straight man to her funny man; I was not too beautiful to be anywhere. To me the world was ugly, and I was good with it. She did not talk about how she hurt. Or rather she did talk about it but she buried it under an avalanche of bits about how she was hurt and deadpan humor meant to make other people say, "Oh c'mon now!" "No, I'm serious!" she would say. "I'm too pretty to be around these roughneck bitches, shoot!" We would laugh.

Now I think about how she felt, not what jokes she made about how she felt. Maybe she was afraid, she was ashamed, maybe she feared for herself and probably more for me. Maybe she felt her life was a failure. How could she let this happen? Why couldn't she get ahead?

It now seems to me that my resentment toward my mother, as valid and righteous as it felt at the time, cannot be decoupled from all the ways I was taught to hate and resent women for all of my life. Everyone told me that my mother was unreliable, untrustworthy, selfish, slutty. Sometimes directly. Sometimes they dropped the hint and let it linger, floated their distaste for her in their turns of phrase.

The thing about being a sensitive, verbal child is that you internalize everyone's feelings and that means oppressive systems take root in you just as surely as the need for freedom from them does. You are a blank thing, permeable and retentive, like those pieces of AI that are turned loose on the internet and learn how to be human only by learning how to be racist.

But in the end, it is not enough to be hurt and to know that you have been hurt. The price of being alive, of being in love, is that you are required to heal.

I brought her back to Los Angeles to live with us. I was short-tempered with her. I found her annoying because underneath everything, I wanted her to apologize for my life or at least acknowledge that I had suffered and that at least some of it had been her fault. She would not. Whenever I brought it up, she would dismiss it with a roll of the eyes and the same *Oh, Carvell, please* that she would give me when I was a teenager and I would hound her about her cigarettes. When you want something from a person that they are not capable of giving you, you become unreasonable and irritable with them, trying to get them to do the impossible. I was more interested in being understood by her than I was in understanding her. More interested in being loved than in loving.

I never knew if she was telling the truth. About anything. A few days before she died, she admitted, "I have a problem with lying." She did not say more about it. She was already drifting in and out of consciousness. She had a seizure. We played music from the gospel station for her. She would talk to people whom she said were at the foot of her bed. She said they were nice, they were welcoming. She said they were everywhere. I imagined festivalgoers at an old-time world's fair strolling the walk with parasols and canes. I wheeled her outside the house onto the porch, where she could watch my kids play. They were three and five years old.

I asked her a question I had wanted to ask her my whole life but had been afraid to. I asked her if the man she said was my father was really my father. We looked nothing alike. She shook her head and laughed. *Oh, Carvell*, she said, *I stopped thinking about that a long time ago.*

I decided that it didn't matter anymore. I decided that nothing mattered anymore, when she lay on the bed with my head in her lap, an oxygen tank next to her. I decided that all I had left for her was love, love that I would use to stay connected with her no matter where she went. I knew she would leave me for a final time, just like she left when I was eighteen months old, just like she left when I was eight. I discovered that any resentment could be let go of at any time for any reason when we are faced with death. I decided that we are always faced with death.

This is why I don't want to write about the people who have hurt me. They are among the dying. I am among the dying. You are among the dying. To be among the dying, and to know it, the feeling that gives you, that is another word for love.

When she took her last breath, I was alone with her. Lee and the kids were at the beach. She just stopped, stopped being. Right in front of me. First she looked at me. Then she looked upward. Then she was not looking at all, even though her eyes were open. I watched her soul vanish. I was holding her, and then I was just holding her body. There was nothing else I could do.

In that moment, the first words that accidentally escaped my lips were:

Mommy. Don't go.

It was funny. Of all the times in my life I wanted to say that sentence, this was the first time I actually did.

Part Two

Stories About God

The Journalist

On a Thursday in Brooklyn, I had just finished interviewing a man who had met Mister Rogers as a child. He was an adult now, a reporter and documentary filmmaker living in the kind of apartment that you're told everyone in New York has but no one you know does. Exposed brick, framed photos of faraway locales, the smell of tea. He padded around the place serving me and the producer with a confident smile. "This isn't much," his face seemed to say, "but it's what I call home." But it was much, a gorgeous loft in a converted chapel, and he knew it. His face somehow also said that. I was interviewing him for a podcast about Rogers, a man I had very little acute interest in before I was offered the gig of hosting and writing. I watched *Mister Rogers' Neighborhood* when I was little. I had seen him in an elevator once in Pittsburgh when I was about nine years old and my aunt took me to the municipal building where she worked. Also, I knew on some level that he was a bodhisattva, but not one I personally cared about. Nevertheless, I took the job because it is my personal belief that you should always spend personal time with a bodhisattva if you can. And also, the money. My fee for each episode was about four times my monthly rent.

The guy told me his story. His parents were journalists in the 1980s, assigned to what was then Communist Moscow. He and his sister were of course two of the loneliest kids in the world, to be so far from what they knew. He described the only toy store in Moscow as an empty room with two or three wooden things in it. That struck me. He and I were roughly the same age. I was not wealthy by any stretch of the imagination growing up. And to be sure, around the time he was whining because his two parents were gainfully employed in Moscow I was probably staying in a motel by the highway in Washington, DC, with my mom and wondering why it was that I was even born. But even still, the one or two wooden toys haunted me. I may have been hungry and unsafe, I may have been with a single mother who did not know how we were going to eat, it may have been that my nights were empty and cold and uncertain. But even I knew that somewhere there were entire buildings filled with plastic toys and that one day I, as a child of America, might have them for myself.

Fred Rogers was visiting Moscow right around the

time this kid was living there with his folks, as part of the cultural exchange programs that were expected to lead to the end of the Cold War. While he was there, Rogers heard there were some American kids who were sad in Moscow because they didn't have roomfuls of colorful toys to look at. So, he made a visit to their apartment. Just showed up one day, knocked on the door, and stayed for dinner. He was wearing his cardigan, probably some eighties-style slacks with a crease in the front and a pretty wide leg, and he was carrying a suitcase with all his puppets in it. And this guy, this adult in front of me in his New York apartment that everyone has on TV but that he had in real life, he was one of those kids. He showed me a picture. There he was, sitting on a drab-looking couch in a stained living room with Fred Rogers on the couch next to him. Both of them were beaming, positively bathing in the light of the flash. Rogers looked like he was just happy to be alive. On earth. In a body. Like this, on its own strength alone, was a cool thing to him. The kid was trying to keep it together. He looked like he had just seen a teddy bear come to life and the teddy bear was fairly cool and chill and so things overall were fairly cool and chill but not really cool and chill enough to take away from the incredible unchillness of the fact that *he had just seen a goddamn teddy bear come to life.*

That Thursday in Brooklyn he showed me this picture and told me the story and the room got golden light from the window and we both got quiet, and everyone got close to tears and the producer sat between us with headphones and a recorder trying to be respectful and unobtrusive with a huge penis-shaped mic very tastefully shoved between me and the guy.

Since we were talking about the goodness of Fred Rogers, since we were beginning to explore the "goodness" of any human as a concept in and of itself, I asked this man if he thought *he* had grown up to be a good person. And if he had, why didn't he, why didn't all of us but especially him since Fred Rogers had actually touched him, spent time with him, picked him out from the rabble, the piles of forgotten children . . . why didn't *he* live like Fred Rogers did? Why didn't we all go around visiting random kids and doing puppet shows for them and taking stands against segregation on TV at great risk to our careers, talking to children about assassination? Why weren't we all the kindest people? And here he got very quiet, because he hadn't expected the question and he didn't know the answer. And this, of course, is my favorite kind of question to ask as an interviewer: the one neither of us could have possibly prepared for.

"I don't know . . ." he said. Then he was quiet some more, after which he said again: "I don't know . . ."

And then he told me that in his job as a journalist he had gotten a scoop where he got to talk to a terrorist who was wanted by the CIA, the African Union, the State Department and had a multimillion-dollar bounty on his head for bombings, murders, maybe a beheading or two, I don't know. And this reporter, in the apartment in Brooklyn that they always tell you people in New York City have, but that no one you know in New York City actually has, this reporter was the only person on the planet who knew where the wanted terrorist was. And this was because the wanted terrorist had taken to calling the reporter in the middle of the night. The wanted man knew he was going to die. He knew he had done horrible things to people. He just wanted someone to talk to.

And what began just as a cool-ass journalistic scoop for the reporter became this other thing, a kind of human experience, a practice of being present. No need to judge. All the judging had been done. No need to teach him a lesson or hold him in contempt. All the people had already been killed. It was the end. It was just time to sit. So yeah, of course the reporter probably had, like the rest of us, gone through life being a little selfish and dishonest, and occasionally fucking people over when no one was looking. He had probably lied to people and maybe even stolen a thing or two. He had probably looked the other way when someone needed help and he didn't want to be inconvenienced. He had probably made a big deal of helping someone not because he actually cared but because someone was watching and he saw the capacity for a spiritual photo op. Surely all those things were true of this reporter because they are true of most of us, I suspect. But in this one moment, at the end of the life of a horrible man who kept calling him in the middle of the night, the reporter suddenly found that he had the ability to sit and be present, and kind, and open. Not to *do* anything, but to be. And he suddenly knew somewhere inside of him that this being, this presence, was a gift. That he himself, even in all his flaws, had the ability to be a gift, to give a gift, and he suddenly knew that every human, even the worst one he could find, deserved at the very least that gift. And he told me that that was one thing he learned from sitting on a couch next to Fred Rogers in Moscow.

By then the room had fallen so quiet that you could almost hear the dust falling to the hardwood floor and simple oak coffee table, gilded, as it was, in the late afternoon light.

The Moon

Once, I was alone on a rock under the moon at Lost Coast. We had started at Shelter Cove and plodded our way down the shore until we found a small inlet in which to camp. I had a job co-leading nature trips for teenage boys who had spent two years locked up for drug and violent offenses. The program was voluntary, and for some events, we could get a whole quorum to come along with us to crack jokes, make a theatrically big deal of how much they were terrified by rock climbing or nature, bugs or bears, but ultimately, after a while, taking to it like a human takes to god. You remember how when the sun went down that night and the sky turned an unforgiving black, every one of us confronted a new fear?

Kids from cities who spent the whole day talking shit

and making everyone laugh grew quiet and reflective, long pauses between sentences, staring into the fire, telling stories of grandmothers who were callous or benevolent, uncles who taught them to drive in busted-down hoopties, little brothers who caught stray bullets, teachers who either loved or hated them unfairly, officers who knew their names from the time they were children, who locked up cousins, beat stepfathers with batons. Life slowed to the pace of gentle wind, its decibels brought down to the distant call of mourning doves in the manzanita brush. People who had spent most of their lives listening to the sound of humans' struggle against human cruelty were now alone with the sound of a darkness so heavy you could feel it. If I could, I would watch this transformation one thousand times, though I watched it only seven or eight. In those sentence pauses I found space for love. Nothing more or less. Just love in a way I had been trained not to love.

One night at Lost Coast we sat by a fire, in a cove, and watched as the sun set and the ocean turned from blue to unrepentant black and then to silver when the moon, disorientingly bright, threw its light directly on us. The tide came in farther than we thought it would. We needed to recamp. We laughed as we pulled up our backpacks and drying socks, bear canisters and Ziploc baggies of raisins and peanuts. I left my socks too close to the fire and they burned through.

Later, when everyone was asleep, I awoke to the moon calling to me from high in its arc, a spotlight forcing my eyes open. As if in a daze, I climbed out of my sleeping bag and carried it with me as I trudged out to a rock that was alone in the sea and clambered to the top of it, probably twenty feet. The tide was out, the path there was wet but walkable. I set up my sleeping bag and a hoodie for a pillow, finding a perfectly shaped divot to cradle my neck. The moon above me, the sea around me, me doing something weird by myself—three of my favorite things, the complete personal trifecta. I dozed off under the sky above the ocean, several stars twinkling, it seemed, just for me.

When I woke up, it was to the very distinct sound of seawater on granite. I heard it before I felt it, just above my head. Enough time for me to have a full and complete thought that said, *Oh. Seawater just landed on this rock. I wonder what is happening.* Then a wave splashed up and over me, landing on my face, soaking my sleeping bag. Foam and salt. Cold and bright. I lay there for another moment thinking about what had just transpired. The tide was on its way back in. There would be more waves. I was cold, beginning to shiver, thinking about death, about what it means to vacate a body, about how weird bodies are. It seems cruel that we are to drag them around through this muck for decade after decade. Having our hearts broken, having guns pulled on us, watching each other die, protesting to no avail. All the while growing slower and creakier and heavier and sloshier and for what? For what? Thought about that way, the wave made more sense than anything else I could think of. It could have taken my soul out of my body and the ocean would have no memory of that wave. That was one tiny wave of one million waves of one million days of one million years.

I climbed back down off the rock. Dragged my wet sleeping bag over to where everyone was sleeping, changed my long underwear, put on a new hoodie, and sat exhausted under the moon, alone with the sound of the waves and several sleeping teenagers and cocounselors until the sun came up. In the morning I told the story, and everyone laughed. I laughed too. But it was weird. Sitting on that rock, shivering and bright, dispassionately contemplating the inevitability of everything, it was one of the few times I remember being, in the purest sense, happy.

The Lightning

I remember seeing a picture of the whipping scars on the back of an enslaved man. His back is to the camera, his left arm crooked, his hand resting on his hip as if mildly exasperated by some foolishness. His face is turned to the left, allowing his profile to be visible. The scars on his back are a helter-skelter pattern of lines, crisscrossing one another in a chaotic violence.

You know the picture.

I've also seen scars made by lightning strikes on the human body, and they appear to me as remarkably similar to the whipping scars, the way each line splits the flesh, cleaving it in two, spreading outward in a fractal pattern of trauma.

The way a thing that used to be one is torn in two.

Violence breaks you; it ends your wholeness and

separates you from where you are one. You and home were one, now you are two. You and safety were one, now you and safety are two. You and yourself were one, now you have been rent asunder and you are destined to spend the rest of your life looking for the part of you that has been taken, looking to be made whole again. At a certain point every love, every loss, every fight and recovery, every step you take toward or away from everything you seek or run from, every rock you climb, kiss you steal, hand you hold, battle you choose, embrace you reject, lie you tell, truth you face in the darkest and loneliest hours of the longest nights, is really nothing more than an attempt to be made whole again, to find what it was that they took from you.

Reunion. To be made whole again.

That is another word for love.

Part Three

Stories About Reunion

The Stars

There are one hundred billion stars in the Milky Way galaxy and there are one hundred billion Milky Way galaxies in the known universe. Humans have been on this planet, one of the eight planets that circle one of the one hundred billion stars in one of the hundred billion galaxies for anywhere between two hundred thousand and two million years.

There are times in my life when I've been outside at night and have been far enough away from traffic lights and strip malls to see more than a few stars in the sky. There are some nights like that when the air is cold and rain has swept away everything in the sky and the clouds have moved seaward on the wind, and the sky doesn't just *contain* stars, it is, in fact, *only* stars. They are a rash, a fabric, a blanket. I make a game of bending back, looking up and then farther back. I keep bending my body back far enough that it becomes a stretch, then a yoga posture, then a trick, pushing against the edge of my form, trying to view everything from the horizon in front of me to the one behind me. And for 180 degrees there is nothing but stars. I've seen this only a few times.

I have been told that the North Star we now know was not always the North Star. Because of the earth's weird occasional wobble in time, the North Star changes about every fourteen thousand years or so, give or take. Polaris, which is our current North Star, is not only the brightest of all the North Stars–in-Waiting, but the truest North among them. It is believed by some that during the era in which Polaris is in its reign as North Star, the evolution of human consciousness makes great advances. We are in the Polaris phase. When Vega, a star altogether dimmer and more off-center, is our North Star, then human consciousness is thought to slow down its growth, and we remain stuck and stale, which is perhaps entirely less painful.

Advances in consciousness are not the same as advancements in technology, though it is hard not to think of them as being similarly linear. What I like about the idea that consciousness can advance and regress is that it suggests that it is not linear, but rather cyclical, maybe even circular. Like the space from one horizon to another, the space that makes a firmament of stars is also curved. I enjoy the belief that most meaningful things come in curves and contain turns. This is one conception I have of a god and also of love: the turning of things. The seasons turn, time turns, the earth turns. My body curves and turns, my youth becomes my age, my wisdom returns me to my childhood. My pain turns into hope and into love, my love into fear and suffering.

The power of looking at stars is that I am looking at the same stars that my ancestors looked at, that people looked at hundreds of years ago, maybe thousands. I also think about the fact that the stars are equally possessed by every people in every place on the planet. There are only a few things that are equally possessed by all people. Death and birth are not. Love and fear are not. Perhaps it is only the stars. I think about the fact that 436 years ago in India someone was looking at the sky and contemplating the nature of existence just as in the land that is now thought of as Gabon 1,317 years ago someone was. In the place that we, for the time being, call Buffalo, New York, 615 years ago someone was doing the same. In fact, in McKeesport, Pennsylvania, where my bike got taken from me by two older kids who punched me and pushed me into the bushes when I was eight, in that land, on that spot, at some point in time, someone stood and contemplated the agglomeration of stars just as I sometimes am able to.

In one thousand years someone will stand where I stood and think what I thought and time will once again have returned to where it is, where it always is, which is the now. Turn and return. This is what I know of life. This is what I know of love.

Once, I was in a hot tub with J.L. We were staying in a house by the beach that her mothers had recently bought.

Old and awkwardly designed, the home stood like a barn on the side of a sunny hill covered with ice plant and solitary windswept cypress trees. I had visited J.L. there a few times, usually for focus and quiet for work. She taught American history at a private school in the city and would go to the house when she had piles of essays to grade from kids who were putting all their effort into being good, getting into elite colleges, either carrying on their family tradition of being in the 1 percent or, in some cases, desperately trying to succeed in order to make good on the promise of their immigrant parents' life-consuming work. The papers were long and required effort. These weekend days were quiet, a fire sometimes roaring, a playlist going, both of us lost in work, only breaking the silence to float lunch plans or make a joke.

In the evening we would pull tarot cards, make dinner, talk about the history of America. She would tell me the story of this or that election, this or that compromise, this or that legal case that laid the groundwork for where we are today. I had learned none of it in school and I was always amazed. We feasted on bread from the Freestone Bakery stuffed with olives and cheese. We had a candle going; ravens and turkey vultures swooped and called outside. The entirety of this country's history, she seemed to think, was defined by one thing and one thing only: white people trying to make sure they were the only people with rights. Every government failure, every form of collective suffering, every inhumanity and violence of this state in this moment, she explained, could be traced back to white institutional cruelty. And here she would produce the citations.

At night we'd sit in the hot tub, silently trying to figure out the meaning of everything. Why are things this way. What can we do. How do you live like this.

One night the stars were so good that I downloaded an app to get to know them better. Just as I had a revelation, a star that I was looking at twinkled and faded and twinkled again. I immediately decided that this was to be my favorite star. It was speaking to me.

The revelation I had was this:

We are made of stardust, but it doesn't matter. The stars don't care, the heavens don't care. No one cares what we do. It sounds like the very high school philosopher realization that we are inconsequential, but it is something different. When you are a teenager and it first dawns on you that we are inconsequential, the next thought quite naturally is "and therefore nothing matters." But in that moment in the hot tub in my midforties, I thought about how many of us are here on this earth. Trying to find words, trying to find love and meaning. Trying to make, create, recover, heal, grow, dismantle, destroy, hold, let go. I thought about the labor activists of the 1920s and the Black revolutionaries who took up arms for my liberation and the liberation of my family in the 1960s and '70s. I thought about my mother holding me in her arms when I was an infant, hoping she could protect me and grow me into something beautiful and powerful. And I thought about the stars and how they don't care about any of it.

And it dawned on me that all we have, in the entire endless universe, is each other.

It doesn't matter to the stars what I do, but it does matter to *us* what we do. We are all we have.

I tried to save the name of the star that twinkled at the exact moment I had this revelation, but the app was new to me. I didn't know how to use it. The next time I opened it, the name was lost. I like to think that it will come back to me one day, maybe in the moment before I die. I just remember that it started with the letter *I*.

There is a picture I keep on my altar of my grandparents attending my aunt Leora's wedding in 1969. They are close in height, my grandfather in a tuxedo and white bow, his face sharp and chilled, his hair close-cropped and still fully in place. His head is tilted slightly back, his chin up as if daring someone to take a swing. There is a dry, rugged handsomeness to him, and he bears himself concretely in his tux. His torso is short and powerful, his head solid and strong as if chiseled out of oak. His look is weary and slightly untrustworthy, his eyebrows cocked toward the camera. I recognize his face in the faces of many of my uncles and a few of my aunts, but his look seems to strain from a different side of the family than does mine, with my soft chin, round eyes, and general chubbiness.

His left hand is across his body resting with a comfortable ownership on my grandmother, who is round and tall in a pink dress that looks like it is meant for a toddler to wear at Easter. The hem reaches the floor, her hands are hidden in white gloves; she is holding a white clutch, and a small bouquet of pink ribbons is around her wrist. She wears a pink veil that covers her forehead, and her cat-eye glasses reflect the lights and hide her eyes. But you can still read her expression, head tilted softly to one side, a broad, proud smile spread across her face.

That woman, the woman in the picture, gave birth to nineteen children. My mother was the last of them, born in 1953, when Grandmommy was, according to records, about forty-eight years old.

I cannot imagine the fatigue, the pain, the resignation, the exhaustion of bearing nineteen children. Of bearing nineteen Black children as the great-granddaughter of enslaved people, in a country that runs on the blood, oppression, and ruination of Black people, on the subjugation and destruction of women, on the theft of land from its Indigenous people. What is an act of motherhood in those places? What is the act of motherhood performed by one single woman over such a long period of time, decades in fact? I close my eyes and try to feel what she has to say to me about it. But I cannot understand her. It is beyond me. My body cannot hold it. My aunts, when I ask them, share only scattered memories, moments of cooking and fighting, belt whippings and interminable lectures on respectability, all of which are recalled as comedy. Grandmother is scandalized by James Brown lyrics. Grandfather is eating an entire sweet potato pie.

It is her face that I have. My mother had it, and my children have some version of it. My aunt Leora has it. It makes me feel we are of the same clan, the People of the Round Noses and Cheeks. We are a soft people, a people who gain weight easily, talk loud, look bright, laugh incessantly, and carry on vividly. I sometimes wonder how far back that face goes, for how many years has my maternal lineage been a round-faced people? Did it come from Noble Mitchell, her father, born in 1885 in Alabama, who lived, as of the 1930 census, in a small brick house in Fairfield that still stands, though now the owners have three Mercedes crammed in the tiny driveway? Or did our face come from Luvonia Mitchell, née Blalock, born in 1883 in Marietta, Georgia, to Rufus and Sophie Blalock, who themselves were born, respectively, four years before and two years after the end of slavery?

It is wild to come from people and yet not to know them at all. It is like being a bug on a stick floating down a river, asking: *How did I get here? Where on earth did I begin?*

How did those round faces look gazing upward at the stars? What did they think? How did they make sense of their bondage? The maiden name of my great-great-great-grandmother, Sophie Blalock, is lost to history. The maiden name itself was not hers, and neither is Blalock. They are both names she was forced to take. Who is Sophie without a last name? Did she, too, feel so alone in the wash of time, unmoored to a place of her own, carried along by violent tides beyond her control? White slavers gave her a name; her husband took that name from her and replaced it with a name that white slavers gave to him.

In my mind's eye, I see her as young, perhaps fourteen, the age of my daughter now, stealing away for a moment among the stars, letting their light bathe her round face with tiny glittery pinpricks as she gazes upward against a night so vast and humid that it feels like she is not outside but inside something, inside a great body, the belly of a beast, the body of a whale. I see her wondering for a moment about why any of us are here, why has life been structured like this? Why are our people confined to this land and place, under the rule of these vile, fearful, angry, fragile, pink creatures? How does she not only make sense of this . . . place . . . but how does she make sense of *herself* in this place?

I lie in silence asking if she can hear me. I offer her the vision of my children as I sometimes see them, falling over themselves in fits of laughter, running in circles in a windy field, refusing order and guidance, drunk on their youth and the bubbling anarchy of tender ages, their faces unbroken by grief and exhaustion, their bodies not yet collapsed under the weight of our cruelty and the sometimes fruitlessness of fighting that cruelty. I show her the way they refuse to listen to anyone or anything, not even their own fears, for too long. It is as if they know they have only a few more years before it all comes crashing down on them, before they become slow and over-taxed and burned-out as we so often are. They ignore us adults because they know what we bring. I want to show them to Sophie. I want her to hear their laughter and screams, the singsong in their voices. I want her to know that we carry her memory in our very cells.

I want to know who she is. Sophie without a name. I look for guidance from her. At times it feels that she is all I have. My life has been confusing and painful and sometimes wonderful, but just as often messy and disordered. Purposeless. I try to heal the disorder with my own two hands, and it feels like trying to arrange the stars. I struggle to clean up the messes I've made, the messes that have been made in me. I try to attend to my growth as one attends to a struggling plant, clipping dead leaves, changing positions in relation to the ever-moving sun. Overwatering and underwatering. I play music for myself, sing songs, ask what I need. I watch my spirit wilt and revive, fall and spring back again. I ask Sophie Without a Name who she is. I cannot find her. I cannot find myself. I am lost and found and always have been. Wandering in vastness and light, weaving between knowing and never knowing, trying to see everything there is to see, trying to be far enough away to understand and close enough to grieve. I return again and again, for after everything else has been lost, return is all I know of love.

The Quit

One night a few years after my mother died, I was on a couch with an empty bottle of liquor and the dishes done. The kitchen had been cleaned. The kids had been put to sleep. The barbecue we hosted that day had been wildly successful. We had plenty of leftovers and the bubble machine was a big hit among the toddlers.

I did not remember drinking the bottle, but the bottle was empty. I was not drunk. I was as sober as I ever remember being, save for a weird sticky feeling I had, which I attributed to too much sun and too much of the lemonade I had been using as a mixer.

I remembered opening the bottle around midmorning just as I began to brine the chicken and dress the ribs. I remembered standing over the grill with a glass in my hand and Lee entertaining the crowd with the story about the time we were in Thailand and I drove a moped off the road. I remembered Lee's mother had been wasted as we were cleaning up, and I thought, *What a shame it is to be retired and drunk at your child's Fourth of July barbecue*, and I vowed once again that I would never do that. But I didn't remember finishing the bottle. It had just turned up empty in my hand.

I thought in that moment of my aunt Trudy, who had cared for me a little bit when I was young. She was older than my mom, short with a bright laugh and a stutter, famous among all the cousins for her cornbread stuffing with pork and browned sage. When I was little, I would sometimes stay at her apartment when my mom was out. It was not a place for kids, with its mirrors and chandeliers, but in it she carved out a place for me. She had a step stool in her kitchen that I used to sit on to watch her cook. She told me it was my special sitting spot. Adults are always telling kids something is special. Kids are always believing it. We watched Hitchcock movies together while she spun stories about her younger days in New York City, dating players for the New York Yankees, partying all night, briefly hanging with the Nation of Islam, living with her younger sister—my mother—as her roommate, having, as she would say, *a ball*.

As I grew older, we drifted. I became a teenager, moved across country. She grew quieter, smaller, and more absent. She drank quietly too. A marriage had failed her, an attempted adoption had gone painfully wrong.

She now lived alone but more safely in a house on the Maryland-DC border that grew increasingly dark and stuffed with cigarette smoke. The last time I saw her I was nearly thirty years old, and we were both drinking. We made small talk in a side room while everyone else laughed and yelled in the living room. She offered me a cigarette and gently chided me for smoking. We had in common that neither of us liked crowds.

She was so much smaller that day than she had ever been, as if she was slowly disappearing, and now here she was, almost finished. I was hurt when she died, but not surprised. I chalked it up to just another one of life's many losses.

I went to her funeral and felt in a daze the entire time. Sitting in the church, watching long-lost friends greet each other, people I hadn't seen since I was little—since all of us were little—people who had laughed and danced and done the Bump and the Rock with You with us in rec rooms to late disco and early funk, tossing us in the air as we screamed and giggled, braiding our hair, laughing and telling us *uh-oh* and *c'mon now* when we dared each other to show off our dance moves for the grown-ups.

I watched them from my seat in the front pew next to my mother and it all felt like I was witnessing a dream from behind a thin layer of gauze. I could not touch anything. I felt only an emptiness, the absence of her, the absence of me, the absence of time and hope and home and safety. And I watched the men hug and the women hug, and I missed how beautiful we all were. I missed my home so deeply in that moment. I didn't know where it had gone or where I had gone. I did not know how to make it back there.

A few weeks after she died, a letter from her arrived in the mail. She had apparently put the wrong zip code and it had taken a long route, but made it to us eventually. With handwriting in the perfect script of a woman trained in 1950s public school, she told me she loved us and missed us and was so pleased to hear about our little boy who had just been born. She could not wait to meet him, and if he was anything like me, he was surely a gorgeous and wonderful little man.

Reading the letter, I thought about my son sitting on her living room floor, as I had, watching Alfred Hitchcock movies with her, asking her about her life in New York City, and for some reason a grief entered my body in that moment that I don't think has ever left. Maybe it was there all the time and the mere act of holding that letter in one hand while holding my baby son in the other just helped me find it. Maybe I had forgotten that when I was a little man, I meant something to someone the way my son meant something to me. I was gorgeous; people wanted to hug me and care for me. I was loved. Maybe I had forgotten that. And being reminded of a love like that at the precise moment you also realize that love is gone forever, maybe that was a grief I didn't know what to do with—that I still don't know what to do with.

It was seven years later that I was sitting on the couch after that Fourth of July barbecue with an empty bottle, having what some people like to call a moment of clarity.

The memory of my aunt Trudy came to me, and I realized that her death was not something she did to herself, and it was not "just another of life's losses." It was something that *happened* to her because after a while the drinking makes up its mind for you and it doesn't matter anymore what you wanted to do with your life. It is too late. It is like a roller coaster that has crested the hill and is only going down. Nothing can stop it. At the bottom of the hill is death. There is no other thing.

I still marvel at the clarity with which this came to me that night. I was not used to there being so few questions. The image of the roller coaster was vivid, as was another image of sand slipping through my fist with greater intensity the more tightly I gripped it.

I realized in that moment that there were only two choices available to me and that I had to decide between them right then and not a moment later. The choices were: stop drinking or die an alcoholic death. There would be no more time. There was no third option. This was the moment, tonight, to either save my life or lose it.

I told Lee in the morning that I was quitting drinking. She did not take it well. We had a pact, unspoken but incredibly strong, where we both agreed that although we had come from alcoholic families, we would break the cycle by drinking so carefully as to never have to quit. Quitting was the nuclear option, the last resort of people who couldn't keep it together enough to enjoy themselves, and we were not going to go out like that. But I had had a moment of clarity and I told her about it, and she quietly acknowledged it, and mumbled, *That's great*, and then a few days later told me she was leaving our marriage.

I didn't know it then, but I know it now: her response was the exact right one. When you lose yourself with someone, you cannot recover yourself with them. Sometimes, it is that simple.

I got sober lying in the fold-out Murphy bed of my studio apartment in the afternoon, wallowing in my own spiritual filth, the blinds drawn shut, watching dozens of episodes of *30 Rock* in a row, smoking cigarettes, eating chips and cookies, nachos and tacos, ice cream and lemonade, falling into a gaping maw of grief so wide it actually impressed even me, who was never impressed by any feelings because I thought I had already experienced every single feeling there was on earth, which up until that point I knew to be: (1) Chaos. (2) My Mother Is Gone. (3) Everyone Hates Me. (4) I Want Something but Can't Have It. (5) We're All Going to Die or Are Already Dying. And (6) Please Love Me. Turns out there were more feelings than that.

I also got sober by hanging around with other people who were getting sober and who were a motley assortment of randos that I found painfully awkward, too quiet or too loud, too pushy or insecure, idiotic, absurd, judgmental, and entirely incapable of understanding my unique situation, which I was quite certain no one on earth had ever experienced before. But I didn't have anyone else to talk to because getting sober was like slowly waking up from a dream, and in the early days of this waking I was groggy and entirely unsure still of who or what had been real and who or what had been imaginary, so I avoided everything and everyone from the dream altogether.

Therefore, all I had left were the randos, and we kept going for coffee or ice cream sundaes or fried chicken at two in the morning, meeting at parks for interminable hikes at 8:00 a.m. And I started seeing the weirdos get better and become normal a little bit, and surprisingly become less annoying, and I saw other people go back to drinking and then die, just up and die, even though it was just two days ago that we were at the Can't Fail Cafe playing "Who Remembers This Eighties Commercial," and he was cracking me up because everything he said was actually funny as shit, and I was just thinking, *I should actually kick it with dude some more, he's actually not that bad*, and now I'm at a memorial service for him and I can't believe I didn't even get to be friends with him long enough to gently suggest that he stop dressing like Guy Fieri. And it was overwhelming, and it made me realize that I literally have control of nothing, like nothing, not even when I'm dead cold stone solid ice hard rock sober, and more importantly that I'm not supposed to have control over anything, and I was never supposed to, and that my whole life regarding that fact has been a lie. The feeling of realizing that the simple, undramatic, desireless truth of it, that was another of the feelings that I didn't know existed.

Still another feeling I didn't know existed was the feeling of sitting at a table with Lee, who had also stopped drinking six months after I did, and formally admitting all the ways I behaved toward her and with her that I was ashamed of, that I knew were wrong at the time but thought were justifiable for this reason or that one, but mainly because I thought something could be both wrong and justifiable at the same time, mainly because for that moment how I felt was how I felt, and how I felt was that it was more important to get what I wanted than it was to truly care for her as a fellow human being with her own couple hundred pages of memoir-worthy trauma and suffering; and to tell her all of that and to watch her nod her head and cry and hold my hand and then to listen for another two hours about how she felt and what my behavior meant to her, and then to hear her admit all the ways she was selfish and cruel and dishonest and violent toward me, ways that I knew, I suspected, but had never heard her admit, and to realize that somewhere in me, in some long-forgotten, vaulted-away place that I did not know I even had, there lived the ability to forgive her for these things because seeing her as a full human outside of me and not just in relation to me also meant seeing the child in her, struggling and afraid, trying to overcome, looking for her own mommy, and I saw that we had been children when we met and that we had tried to love each other and that we were still trying, and it's just that we were still learning what "loving each other" actually, really, truly, genuinely, practically means.

And I didn't apologize in any serious way to my kids because they were too little and fidgety to pay attention to anything like that for any length of time, so I just made my life my apology, my way of loving them and showing up for them and telling them that I was proud of literally every aspect of who they were, and that I was listening to them and learning from them, and just spending time with them, fighting with them, and laughing with them, and apologizing to them when I was wrong or self-centered or short-tempered, and trying every day to give them space to be who they truly and deeply want to be, and watching movies with them, and driving the coast with them, and taking them to the library, which they, and I cannot stress this enough, *sincerely* hated, and going to thrift shops with them, which they sincerely loved, and then the museum, and then ice cream, and then a fight about folding laundry and a clean room and then a question like *Dad, why do they charge money for things people need to live?* and then a board game.

And I tried and failed at love over and over again so many times that I finally thought I might understand it now. I made every dating and sex mistake there was to make. I dated people who I was afraid of and people who were not who they said they were, and people who I could not be honest with because I wanted to please them, and people who wanted to get married to me even though they said they didn't, and people who every single one of my friends told me to block once they heard about what they had done, and people who were not trustworthy at all, and I also spent years not dating and going to therapy and building new friendships with people where there was no threat of sex, just years of going to Target and coworking and running into each other on a sidewalk and deciding to spend the whole day together window-shopping and drinking boba.

The Universe

At the end of my thirties, I was a few years sober and working at a shitty start-up. No offense to the start-up, but for me most start-ups are shitty start-ups, mainly for the way in which they require you to *believe* in what you're doing to compensate for the sheer ludicrousness of it. It wasn't the product or tech that was ludicrous, it was the unadulterated sales of it, the near-religious passion, the way you had to convince yourself, your staff, your funders that what you were doing mattered. *Really mattered*. You couldn't just say, "Yeah, idk, basically we're here for money. We'd like to make some of it, we think this product can make some. But other than that it has no real use, and may even be actively harmful." You had to say, "We're disrupting this, and revolutionizing that, and blazing a trail into this other thing." I found it stupid.

Nonetheless, for a few years I did it. Because I, too, was there for the money. There was not a lot of it, but after fifteen years in nonprofit it seemed like a lot. In the end I didn't make money but I was around money. I was close enough to smell it. I thought if I played my cards right, I could get a little bit of money to fall in my lap. I did not. The cards, turns out, could not be played well by someone who hated the game.

One night while working there, I wrote some text on Facebook about the trial of George Zimmerman for the murder of Trayvon Martin, which I had watched from the start-up offices as the only Black person on the entire floor. That experience was depressing. Alienating. Exhausting. But the post I wrote seemed to touch people. Friends shared it and friends of friends shared it. Sometimes people need words to describe their pain and for whatever reason they can't quite come up with them. I guess that's where I come in.

Eventually a friend asked if *her* friend could put it on her blog. I agreed. I guess the post did pretty well on the blog because more people seemed to be sharing it and I got more friend requests on Facebook, which I was blindly and cluelessly still using then.

Later, the person who ran the blog asked me to write another piece and I did. After it published I forgot about it. Then one of the blog's readers liked it and tweeted about it. She happened to be a retired nineties supermodel with half a million followers. A week later I finally remembered that I had a Twitter, and when I logged on, I found an avalanche of notifications and new followers and lots of DMs, including one from an editor at a music blog who was looking for new voices to break up the monotony of white bros writing about music. I did a few pieces for them, the third one of which blew up and I again found DMs from editors of other magazines in my inbox. For a year, I worked at another start-up by day, parented by night, and cranked out pieces in the wee hours of the morning. I slept an average of three hours a night.

Soon I was offered a gig at a formerly dominant media company that had since fallen upon irrelevancy but now had a grand plan to remake its newsroom image with a mix of veteran music writers and newcomers. I was in the newcomer group. It was a little like being a forty-year-old freshman, but I was down. I've always been down for weird shit, if I thought the weird shit was going to be interesting. They offered me a weekly column for the grand sum of $600 per piece, about seventy-five cents per word, or $2,400 per month. I was a divorced father of two kids in the Bay Area and $2,400 was in no way going to be enough money. But I also recognized that it was going to be difficult for me to do this job and still work at the start-up. It was difficult enough to work at the start-up without this job. I faced a decision. I had to choose.

For days I labored over this, weighing the pros and cons, talking to friends, seeking counsel from mentors, praying, worrying. On one of those days, I came home to find that there was an eviction notice on my door. I had rented my apartment out on Airbnb while I traveled for work and my landlord kicked us out. It hadn't occurred to me that it was against the lease to rent on Airbnb, but it obviously was. Nonetheless, there were probably other factors at play. I was paying $2,000 a month for a place that could have easily gone for twice that. (After I left it pretty much did.) Also my neighbor in the triplex always struck me as a fairly anti-Black dude, evidenced by his initial warning to me and my kids to stay away from the house two doors down because they were "drug dealers" who had "people coming and going all the time." We lived there for three years and all I ever saw was a Black family who had some friends. It was him, I later learned, who complained to the landlord about my houseguests.

In any event the landlord, who had previously gone on at length about how we were the perfect tenants and how she hoped we'd stay there forever, now refused for two weeks to answer a single phone call or email from me. The eviction was sudden and final, no questions asked.* I accepted defeat, recognized that I could in no way afford another three-bedroom in the Bay Area, and made arrangements for my kids to move in with their mom while I took on a less-than-ideal-and-more-dramatic-than-I-had-hoped-for roommate situation across town for $575 a month. Real 1990s prices. The silver lining was this twist of fortune meant that I could take the music news job because my rent was now so incredibly low, even if the place did come with random side-quests like someone who showed up to the house periodically threatening me and demanding money that my new roommate owed them. It was also real 1990s living.

I took the writing gig, and the third piece I published happened to get noticed by the money manager of an NBA player who was thinking about writing a memoir. They contacted me, we began discussions, and a year later we had a book deal in place. The book went on to spend thirteen weeks as a bestseller and ended up on Obama's year-end list.

Meanwhile a person I had dated briefly (things did not end well) invited me on their podcast. I did only the one episode, but the producer that day remembered me and when she got another job, she asked if I'd pitch a project at her new podcast shop. I did and it got made and won a Kaleidoscope Award for excellence in media. Another producer on that show came to me two years later with another podcast idea, which we then made and that show did pretty well too, earning a Peabody nomination. A third producer on *that* show asked if I'd be willing to do a quick guest spot on another podcast about Black parenting that their friend produced. I did, it was fun, and I remain close friends with the host of that show. We formed a connection that day that we have been exploring for years since.

Once, I was telling a very young, very woo-woo friend about my career and the weird series of happenstances that seemed to bring it into being and she said: "Wow. Have you ever thought about how the universe conspired to bring you to this moment?"

The truth was I had not thought about it, at least not in that way. I had thought about my privilege, good luck, hard work, and the occasional leap of faith and following of intuition, but I had not thought about the universe conspiring. But the person on the Black parenting podcast always says this. *The universe is conspiring for your success!* I can hear her voice saying it now, her slight lisp, the singsong laughter in her tone, the Bronx accent that underlies every word she speaks. As nice as that sounded, I can't fully believe that it is true because how do you explain all the ways in which people suffer and are in pain? How do you explain all the times we don't have success? How do I explain the nights I was cold and hungry and did not have a safe place to live? Where was this alleged universal conspiracy then?

It has been years that I've been thinking about this idea, that the universe is conspiring to help me. And would you believe that it was only this morning, when I called this friend—who now lives overseas—just to update them on my life, when it occurred to me what the "universe is conspiring for your success" might mean. If we define success as cash and prizes and goods and money, then hell no, the universe is not conspiring. Capitalism is conspiring, patriarchy and white supremacy are conspiring for sure. But the universe is not conspiring.

But when I think of success as something else it is a lot easier for me to see the conspiracy. What if I think of success as connection? Relationships. Togetherness. The moment in which I speak a truth and you hear that truth and recognize it within yourself, recognize *me* within yourself. The moment in which you tell me who you are, and I see you in a way that makes you feel like a complete and total human being. What an amazing gift, not only to *feel* like a complete human, but to be *seen* as one. When I look at the bizarre arrangement of things that had to align for me to be where I am today, it doesn't seem like the purpose was to have a career or gain followers. It seems like all of these forces made it possible for me to find you. As you are right now. Where you are right now. And for you to find me. Because I think we might need one another.

---

* At the end of two weeks, the landlord sent me an email announcing that she was rescinding the eviction and she was sorry for overreacting. But it was too late. I had already arranged to move into a new place. It was almost as if those two weeks were just there to do for me what I couldn't do for myself. I mean . . . who the hell knows?

The Pandemic

Things became quiet enough that we seemed, briefly, to understand that there was no other place to be, no other thing to be doing. We had been treading and trudging, against and uphill and in opposition to, trying to make enough money for it to work, enough to keep us alive or safe, enough to resist or survive or forget or overcome the suffering and violence we saw before us and felt within us. We had believed that we could not *do* anything about anything because we were kept too busy trying to survive anything, too busy making sure anything didn't happen to us the way it happened to everyone else, or else trying to recover when it did.

But for a few months, things became quiet enough that we seemed to briefly understand that there was something more that we needed to do together, and that it didn't involve shopping, or working, and that self-care might just be a useless and impossible exercise if there is not collective, community care. For a few months deadlines threatened to disappear, waters ran clean, roads become open once more. We were dying or close to death, or rather we admitted that we were close to death. We knew, more clearly, more collectively, than we ever had that we were close to death. We saw that this knowledge might change how we relate to one another, and to ourselves, and to our world. We started to let it. For a brief moment, anyway.

I disappeared into myself and into my home, my plants grew absurdly, I flirted and went on socially distant walks and sat on porches with my best friends. We yelled through masks on their streets, our tales of sex and woe echoing along the duplexes, the sound of the couple in one building over fighting with each other became the music of the whole block. J.L. and I figured out that the reason we can't ever collectively organize in this country is because we were too busy either bullshitting or dealing with bullshit and now that we were not busy who knew what might happen.

It took three months of not working before we saw the largest protests in American history. I was tear-gassed alongside my children. I watched them grow up as silhouettes against the burning of buildings and the explosions of flash grenades. I watched them grow up kettled by riot troops, planning escape routes and meet-up points, hosting marches and collective food drives, distributing flyers, marching to the mayor's house, the police station, the school, the city hall, the courthouse, learning how to keep anonymous when you challenge the authority of the state, learning how to build coalition and community with people who were not exactly like you but who wanted freedom the same way you wanted it. I stopped dropping them off at the mall and started dropping them off at actions and protests and strategy sessions. I did not wait for them to return from parties; I got phone calls at 2:00 a.m. asking me what they should do about having to flee and getting separated from one another on the street while fires burned and they saw someone getting the shit beat out of them with batons.

We sprayed our hands with sanitizer and did not hug and everyone took up roller-skating for some reason, and we laughed about how far we had all fallen and or how much we had returned to where we as humans belonged, right up against death. We remembered that all of human history is just a series of near-death experiences, wars and plagues, and famines, and floods, and that if anything, this pandemic bonds us to everyone who has ever come before us, the way you are bonded with the people who went to the same summer camp as you, because even if you went there in different years, you still almost drowned in the same lakes, threw up behind the same stinky outhouse, and suffered the abuse of the same shitty power-hungry counselors and bullies that they did, even if those bullies came in different bodies or uniforms.

And I talked on the phone with the person I had fallen in love with who lived in New York. We stayed on calls all day, muting each other so we could shit in peace and then unmuting after washing our hands, falling asleep on the phone, listening to each other parent, drive, play video or board games, prep for bedtime, read books, braid hair, pick splinters, calm tantrums, throw tantrums. We stayed on the phone so long that we began to lose the ability to be without each other and when I awoke in the morning it was 7:00 a.m. where I was but already midmorning where she was, and my first blurry views of the world were of her text messages and memes and Spotify links.

And soon it came time for me to risk flying across the country to see her, and I talked with my kids about it, and with Lee about it, and with her about it, and she talked with her kids about it, and her kids' dad about it, and her mom about it. And we all agreed it was going to happen and it would have to be fine. I talked with a friend who was a flight attendant and she told me that it was safer than people thought to be on a plane because of the air-purification systems, but that the airport was the real sketchy spot and I had better mask the fuck up when I was in the terminal. Airlines were selling limited tickets; most were not selling middle seats. I talked with a physician's assistant I knew who told me her entire method of keeping COVID from her family when she returned from the clinic, how she disrobed in the garage, washed her clothes, showered, and sanitized before hugging her children. And Lee asked me if I would be willing to write down all my information for her, and I thought she meant flight info, but instead she meant *all my information* as in passwords, and banking info, and life insurance information. It wasn't as if I was going to die on the plane, but it wasn't as if I was *not* going to die on the plane, or in a hallway of a hospital in New York waiting for a ventilator, and Lee knew this and she also knew that love was worth the risk of dying because by then she had seen me for twenty-three years, she had seen me hold the hand of my dying mother, she had seen me drunk and sober and depressive and elated, she had seen me gleaming in white on the edge of a cliff, the ocean an undulating sapphire below us, the sky unbroken over the sea, saying my vows to her, while our mothers, adorned in their greatest finery, looked on and sent us the blessings of their bodies and of all our ancestors.

She had seen how I grew and beamed and burned and died moment by moment over the years, and even after we were over, she knew about the relationships I had where I could say to her, "I think I might be dating a toxic abusive person," and she could say, "I'm very sorry to hear that, how can I help?" She had seen all of this, and so when I told Lee that I was thinking of going back east to see my love even though it was a pandemic, she simply said, "Yeah. I get that. You should write down your information."

My daughter did not "get that." She yelled at me and cried and told me that I was abandoning the family at the time they needed me most, and we screamed in the car while my son tried at first to keep the peace and then just stopped trying, and I reminded her that for years I stayed at home with the two of them while their mother took work trips for days and sometimes weeks and that it was only fair that I be allowed to go see a person I loved. And my daughter yelled at me, "THOSE WERE WORK TRIPS, DAD. IT'S NOT THE SAME! SHE HAD TO GO!" And I said, surprising even myself, "Work is not more important than love."

It was the first time I had ever truly understood what that means.

The Plants

In New York a winter storm had turned the city
cold and unforgiving, making each journey outside feel
like a chore. Coats and scarves, masks and boots had to
be donned in a lengthy ritual at the doorway. It wasn't
new to me. I grew up on the East Coast, a thing I constantly feel the need to remind everyone, and this is how
I remember my childhood, or parts of it anyway.

I suppose there is a part of me that feels I am not a
complete person, that I won't be seen as my complete
self, if people think of me as a California person, if it's
not understood that I, too, grew up in a place where the
pipes burst in the winter and sometimes school was canceled because it was too cold to be safely outside. I attri-
bute this to a dumb kind of leftover manliness that comes

from a childhood in a rusted steel town where social value was based largely on how deep into the winter season you were willing to play tackle football.

There will always be a part of me that embraces whatever it is I learned by growing up this way, this feeling it gives me that I can, if need be, make myself immune to discomfort, that I don't entirely need warmth or beauty or comfort in order to survive, that I can turn myself into a vessel, free of attachments.

Of course, this is ridiculous. A ridiculous lie. I do need warmth and comfort, just as all humans do. When I returned to California after this trip, I was more delighted than I wanted to admit to see that spring was already in full swing. There were blossoms on the trees, lilies pushing toward the sky; the amaryllis bulb that a friend had gifted me a year and a half earlier was sprouting its flower for only the second time, paper-thin and white, a pink ring making a halo around its starlike shape.

Mostly I am afraid of needing anything that cannot be promised. And knowing that life can promise nothing means it's safer not to need anything. That is why there is a comfort in the illusion of sufficiency. No one can kill me if I'm already dead.

The problem with this, of course, is that you can kill others, and will. Spiritually, emotionally. To allow yourself to be in need is to be connected to the needs of others. To want for beauty is to understand how and why others want beauty. When I was growing up, boys were taught, in so many ways, to believe that the less you needed, the safer you were. But the primary destructive force of manhood under patriarchy is to feed your illusion of safety by putting others in danger.

My experience of being an adult man of the age I am, from the time I'm from, sometimes feels like the experience of taking a long journey across a vast tundra from one civilization to another. Where I am coming from, men are taught control and power, the economics of fear and abuse. Isolation and mistrust. Violence and emptiness. Where I am going, or trying to go, is a place entirely more human, a place where we don't have to be alone to be safe, where we can, quite simply, care with gentleness and strength, vulnerability and honesty, and yes, even need, for ourselves and one another. It often feels like I'm walking this alone, because I don't know where the men are who were raised how I was raised but are trying to become how I'm trying to become.

I guess that's why it feels like a tundra. But of course, even that image seems like some leftover shit from my childhood lessons on manhood.

The amaryllis bulb is so astonishing, how it disappears all year, and then suddenly springs to life unbothered, alive, bathing in its beauty as though nothing else in this relentlessly ugly world, no matter how dark, how cold or cruel, could have possibly mattered in the interim. There is an easy genius to it that, if I'm being honest, I don't entirely understand, but I entirely wish to embody.

My two friends and I all got them at the same time back in December 2019. During COVID, our group chat, mostly held together by monthly outings to the movie theater, had all but died. I recently scrolled through it and saw that the last round of each of us sending pics and updating one another on the progress of our flowers happened not that long ago in the thread. It was February 29, 2020. After that, a few movie suggestions were thrown out, but we could not decide on a time. A week later, everything stopped.

I revived the chat with a picture of my 2021 flower, and doing so gave me a bizarre, subtle feeling of having understood something new about the universe, or at least our journey in it. Steady, beautiful, without hurry or pause, turned toward light, shared with those you love.

The End Again

I awoke one morning about twenty-eight days into the fires, several months into the pandemic, and the sky was a color that no one had ever seen. The entire world was silent with it. I sat in my room looking out of the window for minutes trying to make sense of it.

Something happens when the sky is that color. It bleeds on everything. It wasn't just the sky that was a sickly golden ocher with highlights of gray, trims of burning orange. My whole apartment was that color. The chair was that color, the unread copies of *The Paris Review* that I liberated from a gentrifying café because I felt like the barista was condescending to me were that color. The punctured inner tube I've been planning to patch as soon as I get a patch kit, which I haven't in months, was that color. The oregano plant that seems to survive everything, the driftwood sculpture that Ka gave me before they left Oakland for good to live off the grid, all of it was that color. It occurs to you suddenly that though you thought you owned all these items, you really don't, you are only borrowing them. The sky can repaint them on a whim.

Until this moment climate conditions in my life were a thing you wait out, gear up for, and get over. There's going to be a storm. Now there is a storm. You get an umbrella and maybe a coat that you don't mind getting wet. Then the storm is over, and you clean up from the storm.

But how do you gear up for the sun not rising, the sky being the color of fire? What do you wear to protect your fragile shell of a body from that? You have the scientific explanation. The smoke and ash are trapped above a marine layer that is blanketing the area, thus filtering out the blue light of the sun and keeping the surface-level temperature cool. The lack of warm air creates a lack of wind, which traps the orange blanket above us, unable to move.

Air quality is actually quite good in fact, better than it was yesterday, better than it will be tomorrow, as the carbons and pollutants are kept from us by the marine layer. All and all it's fine. Except for the fact that something subtly and irrevocably changes, shifts positions inside your body, when the sun doesn't come up. You can read that it's just a result of the fires that have come every year since you were a kid but are now coming faster and with one hundred times more force than they ever used to. But the ancient animal within you knows that you are dying and that there is nowhere to run. Nevertheless, you will get out of bed.

I sat on the edge of the bed and it took me about forty minutes to move from that spot. Occasionally I would check the cheap analog alarm clock that I bought so that I would stop looking at my phone first thing in the morning. It didn't work. I still look at my phone every morning for at least forty minutes. Each time I looked, I hoped the clock would have an answer. There's been a mistake, it's actually 3:00 a.m. I am dreaming. Each minute that passed, each tick of the black hand, made it clearer that this was real. The sun was not coming up. The entire land was dark orange and cold.

It was a color that we had seen only in movies about the end of days or futuristic dystopias. The color of a salamander fire, an apricot pumpkin, a vaguely gray sandstone with streaks of ash and dust. There were no shadows. If this was the end, it was a calm one, which is how I always pictured it.

I have waited for the end to come for as long as I can remember. Ever since the grown-ups forbade us from watching *The Day After* on TV, which we instead learned about by having our older cousins describe in vivid detail how the movie depicted a nuclear blast tearing the skin off regular people going about their lives. I've waited for it ever since I got the game *Missile Command* for Christmas in 1983 and worked my little fingers as hard as I could to prevent nuclear annihilation of my little 8-bit city, failing every single time. Later that day we watched a TV special on Nostradamus and how he predicted everything correctly. So of course, when the narrator told us that he predicted that the world would be ended by Middle Eastern men in turbans, and then they reenacted the scene with a bunch of white men in brownface and turbans, I remembered the destruction of my 8-bit city and realized again, on some core level, that no matter what I did, I was just one pixel in a game that I could not keep from ending.

I thought about the end of the world ever since I read the lyrics to Prince's "1999" when I was about seven years old. The sky was all purple, he told us, there were people running everywhere. The song had terrified me, and for years I couldn't separate in my mind the end of the world from the knocking sound of Prince's LM-1 tumbling over the keyboards. I guess in retrospect, if anyone was going to make a song that would make sense during an apocalypse, it would be an impossibly short Black kid from an abusive home in Minneapolis.

I went out to the sidewalk in front of my building. The air was heavy and thick, wet and acrid. I was walking through a bloodred mist. It felt a little like being born, a little like being introduced to hell, a little like a Wednesday out of time. I stood in the middle of the sidewalk and looked at the sky. I could see a man in the floor-length window of the apartment across the street. He was standing in his pajamas, looking down at me. I pretended I didn't notice him. He watched me watching the sky for a few moments, then backed away slowly from the window. I didn't care. Maybe more people should be staring at the sky more often. Maybe it should be weird not to stare at the sky; maybe if more of us spent more time staring at the sky then we wouldn't be here. I needed to go to the ocean. I don't know why; I just know the ocean is where I go to make sense of things. If there was to be any making sense of this, and I was not sure that there was, it would be there.

I went upstairs, got my keys, stopped in my bedroom, and looked again out the window. I thought of my teenagers, who were at their mother's house. They had not lived full-time with me since I got evicted from my three-bedroom apartment four years earlier. My son would no doubt still be sleeping. At seventeen years old he was making himself in my image, which was to say a depressive with compulsive tendencies who stayed up until four in the morning watching videos and perseverating over the state of the world. Trying to find answers, trying to make sense of the senseless, wrestling himself into a state of extraphysical intoxication of burning eyes, the altered state of buzzing numbness. At least this is what I suspected he was doing. It had been a long time since I had walked into his bedroom at night. I saw him almost every day and he would call me regularly to tell me theories about race, politics, revolution. He would call me to ask me why Black people were killed and what we should do to stop it. He sent me memes and TikToks. I hoped this would be over before he woke up.

I knew my daughter would text me as soon as she looked outside. While my son shares his opinions and ideas with me, my daughter shares only her anxieties and triumphs. She reaches out to me for math help, questions about her world lit class. She calls me to tell me she met a cool older girl who is also an activist, someone she can look up to. She asks me for advice about what to say or not say to KQED reporters emailing about the protests she's putting together. She calls me about anything Black. Black student union, Black politics, Black music, Black movies. Racist teachers, sketchy cops, white men who give her weird vibes. But most of all, she calls me to tell me she's afraid: of the future, of not getting into college or getting into the wrong one, of kidnappings, sexual assaults, police surveillance. These, of course, are all smaller fears because we all know the big ones are too magnificent, too irreversible to mention. We know the sky is burning. We know our country is killing us. We know men are a violence and we know whiteness means to destroy us. We don't talk about these things anymore. What is there to say? I don't want my children to wake up today. I don't want them to see this. I don't want anyone to see this. I want to take the weight of this entire destruction on my back and carry it for the sake of everyone I love. Maybe that is why I feel like I must get in my car and drive alone into the crimson without calling or texting a single person. It is a stupid impulse but one I can't find it in me to resist.

In my car, I turn on the windshield wipers, and ash flies in every direction. I roll down the windows. I always roll down the windows when I drive. It is a mundane act like all the other mundane acts I undertake when I drive somewhere: starting the engine, pulling out of my parking

space, making the U-turn on my wide street to head toward the freeway. Today they all feel like caricatures of
themselves. I am not making a U-turn, I am making a
U-turn at the apocalypse. At the intersection before the
big road, the road that makes me feel like I'm finally en-
tering the world, there are no cars. I pause longer than I
should at the stop sign. There is no one behind me. I realize I could stay here forever, and in that moment, I feel
like everything is finally over and the end has, at long last,
finally begun.

The oddest thing about all of it, the thing they don't
tell you about that day, the thing you cannot imagine,
is the cold. There were fires. But the air was cold.

I drove across the bridge; the sky was not alive. The
streetlights remained on all morning. Pictures started ap-
pearing on social media. We were all posting, trying to
convince our friends and families in other parts of the
country that this was what it looked like. But no picture
made sense. Everything looked like a filter. It is too late in
our human history to be moved by a photo because every
moment has been photographed and every photograph
has been seen. What was the difference between my
photo taken on the Bay Bridge at 9:45 a.m. with the lamps
on and the sky not alive and any other moody photo with
a filter? There is none. I wanted the photos to scream.
Please see us, please notice us, please see that we are dying. Not just here, but everywhere. You are dying. They
are dying. It's just here we are seeing it first. It's just that
the earth has reversed direction and California is now
the first state to experience the nighttime.

I listened to Mos Def's *Black on Both Sides*. I don't remember choosing that album. I just remember that somehow it was playing in my car. It was an album I was obsessed with for a year in 2000. Back then I played it every day on the commute to and from my job at a community gardening organization in the cassette deck of the red Toyota pickup truck that Lee and I had inherited from her father after he drank himself to death at the age of fifty-one. The car was in pristine shape. He had not driven it in over a year because his license was revoked due to multiple DUIs.

I had met him once, about four months before he died. He was a small, soulful man with a spectacular black pompadour and a bushy mustache with a great well of grief and love behind his eyes. He was always wearing denim, his high-waisted bell-bottom Wranglers and chambray pearl-snap cowboy shirt fitting him as if he were born wearing this outfit. He couldn't have been taller than 5′5″. He had been raised poor in the desert, one of twelve children, living in a trailer, and his face looked like the land he came from: leathery and brown, his nose bulbous with drink, his hands thick and veiny. He had gone to Vietnam when he was nineteen and returned with severe drug and alcohol addiction as well as a not insignificant case of agoraphobia.

He died one day after work, drink in hand, in the tiny studio apartment in Burbank where he lived because it was within walking distance to the Weber's bread factory where he, like all his brothers, was a union baker. The apartment smelled of Naugahyde and cigarettes, the carpet warm and thick, the vertical blinds permanently closed. We were twenty-five years old. Lee was his only child and his next of kin, the only person who could get his body out of the morgue. We were not in America the day he died; we were in Southeast Asia at a nearly empty guesthouse in a Laotian border city. We traveled for thirty-two hours to make it home, planes, trains, cars, tuk-tuks, motorcycles, boats, until we arrived on the ground at LAX and went directly to the funeral home near Joshua Tree, where he was to be buried. Afterward we lived in his apartment in Burbank for several months working at competing corporate coffee chains on the same block while she waited for his pension check to come through so she could pay off her student loans. We were confused and aimless. We were not yet married.

We had been touched by death and did not know what to do with it. Almost none of our friends, who were also twenty-five, reached out to Lee. They did not know what to say. They did not yet know that you don't have to know what to say when you are supporting someone who is grieving. There is nothing to say. There is only presence. There is only love. There is only the looking into one another's eyes and saying, with your whole chest, your whole soul, *I am here.*

We could not return to New York. It was the summer of 2000 and the NYPD had killed Patrick Dorismond, sodomized Abner Louima with a plunger, shot at Amadou Diallo forty-one times while he was holding a wallet in front of his apartment. I remembered the Crown Heights riots from my childhood, and I felt like New York

City was due for a cataclysmic event. I argued against going back. Lee agreed and we ended up in Oakland, where an actual voice from the heavens, the only one I had ever heard before or since, spoke to me on a Saturday afternoon at dusk and said, *You can get healthy here*, and my first thought was, *Wow. I didn't even know I was sick.*

Mos Def played in my car. I was crying. It was "Mathematics," the DJ Premier–produced track with a beat that—forgive me for saying this—was never my favorite Preemo beat, even though Preemo himself has called it one of his faves. I don't know. I've always thought some of this album, beat-wise, was just . . . you know . . . *okay?* Now that we're all dying, I guess I can admit that. Anyway, I'm sure Yasiin Bey is probably a complicated person who has most likely been problematic in some ways, but I also know that when someone can say lyrics like, *Sixty-nine billion in the last twenty years spent on national defense but folks still live in fear*, I know I can trust them with this moment, the moment when the veil is lifted. There are artists who can see on the other side of the veil and Yasiin Bey is one of those artists and it's probably why he doesn't talk a whole lot now. It is hard work to see what exists on the other side of the veil. Exhausting. Overwhelming. *So much on my mind that I can't recline, blast the holes in the night till she bled sunshine.* My son and I used to bond over Mos's "Auditorium" verse. *The way I feel, sometimes it's too hard to sit still / Things are so passionate, times are so real.* It seemed to describe him perfectly.

I finally arrived at Ocean Beach. I don't know why I

expected the water to have an answer but all it held was the itinerant vastness of the question, the oblivion spanning forever into the horizon and beyond. Concrete seawalls covered in graffiti. That was disappointing but not surprising. But there were many of us here, probably looking for the same answers to the same questions. We had gathered there, hundreds of us by the looks of it, standing along the length of the beach from Sloat Boulevard all the way up to the Seal Rocks, all doing the same thing. Staring. Standing. Hands on hips. Shaking our heads. Taking out our phones, taking a picture. Looking at the picture. Looking back at the sky. Shaking our heads. Hands on hips. Walking a few paces. Repeating. Repeating. Repeating until we finally realized, one by one, that no sense was to be made of this. After which we got in our cars and drove away.

Once, when the kids were little, we took them to see the elephant seals at San Simeon, thousands of them piled upon one another, rolling and mewing against the surf. You could walk right up to them if you wanted to, but of course you're not supposed to, and it wouldn't make a lot of sense to. Yet the desire is there. Not to disrupt them, more like to join them. Still to this day I find myself thinking about what it would mean to give it all up, to be free from the trap of being a human, which means being tied to our collective cruelties and mistakes and illnesses, having to fight for every moment of liberation, devoting an entire life to trying to triumph over the death that surrounds you and lives within you, only to finally realize at the end that no matter what work has been accomplished, there is no better answer than to look out at the sea with your hands on your hips and shake your head at what we've done. Maybe the elephant seals have already made peace with this.

It was lightning that started the fires, which is remarkably rare in the Bay Area. Even more rare is dry lightning, which is what was happening early in the morning on August 16. I awoke in the middle of the night and watched the storm from my bedroom window. It was the first anniversary of the first night I spent with the person I love in New York. On that night the moon over Washington Square Park had been so absolutely stunning, so wet and libidinous looming over our first kiss that I took a picture of it, which I later had printed and framed above my desk. Every time, it seems, something important is happening in our relationship, there is also something important happening in the sky. I know exactly how these two things are related but I simply can't explain it. If I could it wouldn't be true.

There was nothing left to do. I drove home. I took another video. I sat on my bed. Later that afternoon I met up with an old friend who I call the Artist down by the Berkeley Marina. It was still not safe to be inside with someone. The Artist is another person who can see beyond the veil. I felt blessed to be able to spend this day with her. We sat on a bench. She said, "Well. Here we are." "Here" being the collapse and catastrophe that she has been talking about since the very moment I met her. I said, "Yes, here we are." And we realized there was not much left to say. Eventually we decided we would take the risk of holding each other, even though we were on a bench, even though it was COVID. Even though . . .

Every once in a while, I am struck with a full sense memory of what it felt like on that day. The wetness of the air, the deep quiet, everything without an echo as though we had somehow surpassed the concepts of space and distance themselves. The vastness of it, how the orange sky covered everything there was to cover with no escape, no other world to go to. The isolation came later, the stunning feeling of loneliness you had when you realized that people the whole world over could know from the ceaseless Instagram posts what the end looked like but would never know what it felt like, that people the whole world over were still operating under the idea that life was continuing, that the world was true and lasting, which of course it might be. Who knows? It is, in fact, the not knowing that is the death.

Sometimes in the middle of a quiet afternoon, when I am sitting on my roof smoking a cigarette, reading a book under a tree, all those feelings and senses come back to me with a force that is unexpected and hard for me to fully comprehend, a force that breaks down the wall between past and present, between this moment and all the moments that ever or never were. Those memories take over whatever moment I'm in, covering all things with a fierce and unmistakable sense of isolation and loneliness.

But that's only sometimes. Mostly nowadays, it's all forgotten. A weird blip in an otherwise chill California life. People are walking near the lake, families are playing, children are biking, their little helmets askew. It is a perfect seventy-one degrees and I am sitting under a towering redwood tree on the campus of my daughter's school, a school that has been closed for almost a year, a redwood that kids have been sitting under since 1908. The grass is moist, a shocking iridescent green. I love this place and this time. I love this shadow and the canopy of branches above me. Which makes sense. The more real the end of things is, the easier it is to love them.

The Bread

Once, it was raining and it was cold. I was sad.
Maybe not sad, but grieving. I don't know why, but then
again you don't have to give a reason for grieving, do
you? Grief has nothing but reasons. Tears were sitting
in my chest, the weight of the sky heaving upon me. It
was cold in my apartment. I was under the weather.
It was raining, which is increasingly rare in these parts.
All in all, it was a wonderful day.

I had work to do, I'm sure of it, but after I had dropped
my kids off at school it became clear to me that this was
a day in which no work was going to get done. Instead, I
was going to make bread.

I started looking for music to listen to while I baked
and landed on Solange's *When I Get Home*, an album
that I somehow never got around to giving a thorough

listening to when it dropped. I poured the flour, measured the water, cracked the egg. I listened to the music. I kneaded the dough and saw things she imagined. She repeats this phrase—*I saw things I imagined*—over floating synthesizers that I read somewhere were inspired by Stevie Wonder's deeply slept-on 1979 literary soundtrack *Journey Through the Secret Life of Plants*. Like Wonder, Solange uses repetition frequently on the album, working incantations over bass motives, calling in memory, ancestry. These sound like New Agey concepts but they are not. In fact they are as old as we are.

I warmed the milk, measured the honey, proofed the yeast.

People did not / do not like *Journey Through the Secret Life of Plants*. It is a double-length album with twenty tracks, only two of which have over a million listens on Spotify, a very low number for Stevie Wonder, especially when you consider that the songs on *Songs in the Key of Life* have over 800 million listens combined. I suppose for some *Secret Life* is just too weird, too instrumental, not groovy enough, not enough to grasp on to. It is not enough of an action, you cannot play any of it at a wedding reception or at an NBA game. Instead it is a meditation.

Solange takes this meditation and puts it on the back of just a little bit of restrained moving and shaking, a bit of head-nodding, some grooving and a polyrhythm or two, which probably makes it a lot more approachable for a lot of people. And that's fine. That's great. I love *When I Get Home* more than I love most contemporary musical works.

Listening to the album, baking bread, reading. The book in my hand was a collection of letters between Pat Parker and Audre Lorde. The two authors struck up a friendship and remained in touch via letters from around 1974 until Parker succumbed to cancer in 1989. Their communications were mundane and profound, a time capsule of modern life in the late twentieth century, wherein they discussed feminism, whiteness, brussels sprouts recipes, poetry, publishing, money management, relationships, adoption, parenting, plants, weather, countries visited, lectures given or received, and how each of them owed the other a phone call. And as the letters progressed, they, of course, talked more of death and love, fear and darkness, light, purpose, and regret.

Because I can't help thinking about how everything relates to me, I noticed that they began writing to each other the year that I was born and continued until I was in the ninth grade. This, in fact, was one of the reasons I loved reading about these two women, both of whom were around my mother's age, and could have, in some parallel universe, been my family. Sometimes it feels like they are. I guess there is a small part of me that wishes they were, that wonders what it would have been like to be raised by people it seemed might understand me as I wish to be understood: as a writer, a melancholic, a thinker. Maybe I *was* already understood that way, but longing for what I already have is part of my melancholia. Maybe I will be forever longing, because longing is forever. I suppose it's not unusual for kids to fantasize about having famous parents. It's also pretty on brand for my fantasy of famous parents to be Black lesbian feminist thinkers and poets from the seventies and eighties, and I definitely mean that as a compliment to myself.

I've been finding a lot of solace in the work and art of Black women from the seventies, eighties, and nineties lately. Kathleen Collins, Edwidge Danticat, Jamaica Kincaid, Grace Jones. I recently went down a pretty significant Donna Summer rabbit hole, inspired by hearing for the first time her 1981 cover of Jon Anderson and Vangelis's "State of Independence," a song that is weird and expansive, arty, hopeful, and hokey in precisely the way that only early eighties art pop could be. The track is vague and poetic, as heavy on one-world-isms as it is on synths, which is no surprise as it was produced by Quincy Jones, who at that time was beginning to fully inhabit his post-disco, post-jazz, West Coast highbrow-pop influencer persona. Donna Summer's backing vocalists for the track were composed of—and I'm not kidding here—Michael Jackson, Lionel Richie, Dionne Warwick, James Ingram, Kenny Loggins, and, yes, Stevie Wonder. If nothing else this was clearly a trial balloon for the "We Are the World" sessions, which would happen less than two years hence. Brian Eno called Summer's "State of Independence" "a high point of twentieth-century art," which should impress you if you happen to be into co-signs from esteemed white men.

All this studio firepower makes me think that there was a point at which everyone agreed that Donna Summer was the artistic future, which, in turn, makes me wonder why it is that by the time I was introduced to her, pretty much all anyone told me about her was that she was a "Bad Girl" and the "Queen of Disco." There is of course a not-so-subtle misogynoir laced into how I came to understand which artists mean what—a deeply entrenched hierarchy of things: If a white man did it, it was art, it had substance, it was academic and philosophic. Even if it seemed silly, it was purposefully so. It was a commentary on silliness. But if a Black woman did it, no matter what it intended to be, it was always going to be received as pop, R&B, party music, sex appeal, and disco. It could be *awesome*, *amazing*, *so good*, *the shit*, but it could never be substantial, meaningful, prestigious. Art made by Black people, and specifically Black women, was almost always treated as colloquial, as folk art. Brian Eno gets to be called a "musical theorist" for what? Because he had enough socially induced hubris to frame his personal thoughts as intellect? I'll bet Donna Summer had some pretty damn interesting theories of music, too, when you got right down to it.

This is what I thought about as I made bread, listened to Solange, read the letters of Parker and Lorde, a significant portion of which were to do with the struggle of collecting resources in exchange for their brilliance and labor. Lorde was experiencing some relative level of success. Parker was still trying to break through. Lorde was constantly offering Parker help, motivated, it seemed, by the belief that she needed to spread the wealth and pull a sister up whenever she could. Problem was there was not a lot of wealth for the spreading. (An endlessly entertaining thing for me is, in the book, how both Lorde and

Parker constantly refer to money as "bread." I don't know why but it just makes me smile. The footnotes are a treasure, too, so much wonderful minutiae about the queer local history of Oakland, special shout to the lesbian softball league that apparently played at the park around the corner from my house.) The amount of money Lorde was making from her conference lectures and small university press book deals could not have been substantial, or at the very least certainly not commensurate with either her fame or her impact on our way of understanding the world. Yet there she was behaving as though she had hit the super lotto and was going to take care of her entire hometown. It makes sense. It must have felt like a lottery to have your words listened to. When your oppression is communal, your liberation must be as well.

This, of course, is what was missing from the work of many of the white artists I was introduced to in college, artists I was told were complicated and deep, layered thinkers making nuanced and intelligent work that would stand the test of time. There may have been prestige there, but there was no celebration, no joy in the mere fact of having made it.

When I think of Lionel Richie, Diana Ross, Michael Jackson, Quincy Jones in a studio in LA, I'm sure they were obnoxious West Coast celebrities on some level. But I also know there had to be a fundamental joy there. Lionel Richie was born in 1949 in a segregated Tuskegee, Alabama. Michael Jackson was one of nine kids in an abusive working-class home in Gary, Indiana. Stevie

Wonder and Diana Ross were from working-class families in Michigan. Quincy Jones was the son of a carpenter on the South Side of Chicago. These people had all made it, and in so doing, they had not just personally done well for themselves, they had done well for their people. They had expressed their souls, they had excelled at their craft, and those expressions had moved the world. There is a fundamental celebration that comes from that, from surviving what you were not meant to survive. I know this because I saw this in my own family. The way my aunts danced in the rec room of their suburban home as if we had all won the lottery by simply having a room to dance in.

A friend told me once the mildly harrowing story of being locked out of her new apartment. Moments later, through sheer happenstance, she ran into a friend who had a lockpicking kit with him, and her day was saved. She said that for the rest of the afternoon she was walking around with what she called "found-wallet syndrome," a feeling that something good had happened to her, when it could be just as easily argued that what took place was that something moderately bad had been partially avoided. For some people, avoiding something bad *is* a stroke of fortune.

I related to this. On some level, I live my whole entire life with found-wallet syndrome. The mere fact of having a home, a bed to sleep in, being alive and relatively healthy, to have loved ones, to have you reading this text even as you are in this moment, to have a space in which to make bread, listen to music, and even grieve . . . to me these are all found wallets. I hope they always will be. This is one of the ways I understand love. Love is simply the feeling that I am grateful to be here and I am grateful you are here too, even if you're on my fucking nerves, which to be honest some of you are.

One impact of a society that gives some people an unquestioned right to all the resources and power is that it creates out of those people a population who cannot understand the sheer and simple love of being alive, the love of gratitude, the love of satisfaction and serenity. Everything is too little for them. The world is never enough. There is not enough action. The mere act of being is not meaningful for them. It never can be.

Sometimes I think our society will be forever lost until we are no longer ruled by people who feel this way. Or until they, too, lose enough to be grateful for the mere fact of being. That may be painful. That may be right.

Making my bread, listening to Solange, the rain dancing ever so lightly on my kitchen window. I know you won't believe this, but nearly two years later, I still think of that as one of the single greatest days of my ever-fading life.

The Beauty

I write about beautiful things because I live in
an ugly place in an ugly world. Where every corner I pass
has the story of a Black person's murder written upon it
and then erased, where men broke into my daughter's
high school in ski masks once and she told me about it
laughing, where a child I took with us on family trips and
hosted at sleepovers just tried to commit suicide by over-
dose at sixteen years old, where many of the people I loved
are in caskets, where we are surrounded by death, not just
death, but allowed death, encouraged death, blood rite,
sacrificial death, no-one-cares death, the death it takes to
keep America America-ing.

I write about beautiful things because I live in a country that has tried to kill me and every single one of my

ancestors. Every single one. Continues to try. Will never stop trying.

I write about beautiful things because someone told me once that when I hear poetry on the wind I am really hearing the voice of my great-great-great-great-grandmother, and even though I didn't particularly like the person who told me that, I don't think they were wrong.

I write about beautiful things because just like I know that people I don't like can offer something valuable, I know that a land I don't like and a place I don't like can offer something beautiful.

I write about beautiful things because I have learned to love things that I don't like. I have learned, even, to see god in them.

They say that religion is for people who don't want to go to hell and spirituality is for people who have been there and don't want to go back, so I write about beautiful things because I don't want to go back. Because my entire life is in bonus, an exception. Because even though I have every right to be here, I also have no right to be here. Even though I should be here, I really and truly should not be here.

I don't write about beautiful things as advice. I don't want to, nor do I care, if anyone else finds things beautiful. I do not write about beautiful things because I think that's what everyone or anyone else should be doing, or thinking, or feeling. I don't write about beautiful things because I don't know that there are ugly things.

I write about beautiful things because my boyhood

was all about learning violence. Understanding violence. Surviving violence. Being taught violence. Worshipping those who could do the best violence. Teaching ourselves to receive the most violence. Never talking about violence because talking about it was soft. Memorizing violence like a song, a video game you learn to play, a movie you watch over and over and over again so many times that you know every line of dialogue and you repeat them to yourselves while you are alone in the shower, naked and wet and unprotected.

I write about beautiful things because once when I was fifteen I came out of the shower wet and naked and unprotected and they were beating Rodney King on television over and over and over and over and over and over and over again and my mother just stood there and cried. And another time when I was fifteen, I came out of the shower wet and naked and unprotected to find two plainclothes LAPD officers standing in my living room with my 5′4″ mother in handcuffs, her arms behind her back, and they told me they were taking her away because she wrote a bad check to buy us a bed to sleep on, and then they said, "You'll be alright, right, man?" and they left with her and I was alone.

I write about beautiful things because believe it or not that was not the last time I would see my mother in handcuffs. The next time was when I was thirty-one and she was fifty-one and we had ten officers pointing loaded weapons at us because we were house-sitting for a neighbor and someone on the street called the police because they saw "two big Black men in the house and they got scared."

I write about beautiful things because my mother was still 5′4″ tall that night.

I write about beautiful things because beautiful things were what I needed when I was young and alone, because beautiful things give me just the tiniest bit of gender euphoria, which I know somewhere deep down I will have only a very little bit of access to in my life, so I take each opportunity to experience it as exceedingly precious and meaningful.

I write about beautiful things because I was randomly listening to the actual terrestrial radio—KPFA, our endearingly low-budget absurdly leftist local station that I will never stop appreciating and supporting even with all its problems and foibles and cringes—and when I tuned in, it was in the middle of an episode of the Asian activist show *APEX Express*, and Lani Ka'ahumanu was telling stories about being the person who got the *B* added to LGBTQ and about doing safe-sex comedy demonstrations in the eighties complete with live fucking, and who—in talking about the complexities of being bisexual in the eighties in radical lesbian spaces—said this wonderfully simple thing: *And I think it is complex, but things don't get complicated if you stick to the truth of who you are and your stories, and stand by that and demand respect, demand and command respect.*

And the other guest was Jayda Shuavarnnasri, who said this wonderfully true thing: *It's just that everything is fluid and radical honesty is at the center of it all. My relationship to my body, my sexual desires, my relationships to people are all fluid and ever-changing, and they're never actually going to be like one boxed thing I could feel really I could be. I'll say that I'm a super sexual person one day, and then feel like I'm not, feel zero desire for sex the next day and let that be okay.*

I write about beautiful things because when I hear these people talk it feels like they are saying things that my deepest essence has been wanting to scream about for decades, and hearing it outside of myself is both a relief and a kind of torture because I want to be heard screaming, YES, YES, ME TOO, and I want that scream to be answered but it cannot be because I am in several ways alone. So, I write about beauty because it is my soul's way of quietly whispering onto the page, *Yes, yes, me too*, and daring you to do the same.

I write about beauty because what has been done to me and to us is exceedingly unbeautiful, and if I don't counter it, it will eat me alive. It has tried. It tries every day.

Some days it comes incredibly close.

I write about beautiful things because everyone tells me beautiful things are not important and it makes me afraid that what I'm doing is useless and who I am is useless, but I remember that I hear beauty on the wind when I listen and that it just may be the voice of Sophie Without a Name, and who would I be if I did not give every part of myself to her call?

I don't write about beauty because I don't know ugliness. I write about beauty because I know ugliness too well.

The Sex

I went to Orange County to interview an athlete for a magazine. It was fine. Joyful even. He was beautiful and ebullient, full of himself, a bit of a SoCal bro in a Black man's body but at a small enough dose to basically constitute good vibes. He had brought his girlfriend to the interview, which I did not expect. She was white, quiet, and thin with long hair front curled, center parted, and a full face of makeup, a silky tank, wedges, and jeans. She looked like she might be young. It gave me pause. I wasn't sure how the fact of her being there should or should not play into the story. I never saw her posted on his social, and he made no attempt to include her in the conversation. She looked at her phone much of the time. The whole thing made me uncomfortable. At a loss for what to do about it, I ignored it altogether, plodded along with my questions while he talked for ninety minutes about his grievances and struggles and successes.

Toward the end she spoke up and I realized that she was an athlete too, and that the real reason I had ignored her was because I thought that my magazine would have wanted me to ignore her. If I had not been there for work, I would have directed questions to her, found out who she was, how she fit into the conversation, what she thought of everything. Then I realized that my editor had never actually said, "Oh, by the way, if he brings a girl with him and introduces her to you as his girlfriend, whatever you do make sure you don't ask her any questions." Ignoring her had, in fact, been my decision. It was me who reasoned that because he was the one on the cover, because he was the person they called me up and offered me money and paid for my hotel, flight, and car to go talk to, that he was the only important one. I didn't think he was the important one. I just assumed everyone else did, and so I behaved accordingly. That's the thing about importance. You can end up treating someone as important just because other people do, no matter what you yourself actually think.

Back in the car, with the interview secured on tape and fully backed up, I drove. I was in a convertible, which had come to me through some kind of clerical error at the rental counter. I was restless in the way that Southern California sometimes makes me, the golden light so pretty as to almost be offensive, the hum of traffic like an ocean, the onslaught of memories. Sex and guns, skateboards and buses. Jimi Hendrix and Sonic Youth. Wide boulevards on fire.

I drove and drove more. The top was down, the dusk was still an hour off. I would be headed back to Northern California in the morning. It had been a long time since I listened to Frank Ocean. I let there be long pauses in my listening to Frank Ocean because there are long pauses in his making music. He makes music like an absentee lover who breezes in and out of town but always calls you when he's around and you always make time for him and it's always worth it. I had to turn it up to full volume to compete with the wind and the noise from the freeway. I was a cliché. A queer Black man driving through SoCal with the top down listening to Frank Ocean. In his feelings. I didn't care. There was light traffic headed north on the 60. I had not cut my hair in over a year. I had decided that I may never cut it again, in love as I was with the idea of my own length, beauty, and power. Recently I had taken to wearing bandanas folded and wrapped around my head like an extra in an eighties gang movie. I had become enamored of the look. I found it exceedingly gay. I took a selfie while I drove, the sky above me. I sent it to someone on Grindr who had asked for a face pic. "Damn. Ur Cute," he replied, and I left him on read.

Traveling northward from the Chino hills was like traveling through my adolescence, through the places where kids I went to high school with lived, places that felt to me like the dry and abandoned outskirts of Los Angeles County. Suburbs where the asphalt burns and nothing grows higher than a bush and the Mexican kids and the white kids didn't seem that different from one another because everyone was into either the Cure or the Smiths or Siouxsie or Depeche Mode, and they were on lots of drugs and felt angry and isolated and reckless.

I passed the apartment where my high school prom date lived with her mom in a nondescript complex. She was quiet and wildly intelligent and had the misfortune of looking like what they used to call a blond bombshell. She didn't talk to many people at school. In response everyone made up rumors about her so that they could control the version of her that existed in their minds. Boys traded tales of her sightings around the hallways, recalling to one another what she wore and how her breasts looked in it. She was rumored to be dating a thirty-five-year-old man who worked at a diplomatic post, a story I dismissed as absurd when I first heard it, but one day he showed up to pick her up in his champagne-colored sedan and we all saw him. He was balding. I didn't know this was rape. I thought this was just another thing about her that made her fascinating and elusive, like she was a spy working undercover among us children. When she asked me to prom, we barely knew each other, and it was one of the first times she had ever spoken to me. I hastily agreed. She then said, "Good. I've never fucked a Black guy before," and made me feel sick. Disoriented. A whiplash so sudden that I decided that the best course in that moment was not to acknowledge it at all. She was a year above me. Everyone wanted to get with her. She was dating a thirty-five-year-old. I did not know I could say no to her.

Prom was whatever; dinner on Melrose was memorable because it was the first time I paid money to eat in what I thought was a fancy restaurant. We ended the night with sex in the back seat of her car, which she parked on a side street in front of an elementary school around the corner from my mother's apartment. I didn't understand what we were doing while we were doing it and I didn't understand it afterward. I just knew I was doing what I was supposed to be doing. She said something about feeling "filled up" by me. Her words felt hollow and rote, like she was reading from a script she had barely glanced at and didn't think was particularly good.

I forced myself to smile about it when I walked up the stairs to my mother's home, trying to inhabit every movie image I had ever seen of "Just Got Lucky Guy." Trying to whistle. Doing a little spin. But honestly, I didn't feel like I got lucky. I felt like something important had been unaccounted for in that harried back seat sex, something had been lost or taken away, something I had no idea how to identify, much less how to get back.

Now I was at West Covina, where the boy who was my high school best friend and my lover lived. We used to drive around the valley in his economy car singing at top volume along with corny rock operas while he avoided talking about his abusive family except in the most random of moments, like while we sat on the bench outside the Taco Bell on Moorpark eating thirty-nine-cent burritos, and in the pauses during which we chewed he would just bring up an act of violence that he had endured. I loved him like I've never loved a man before or since. We did everything except kiss, which still to this day makes me incredibly sad. I will probably never love in that way again because I will never be that young again. I am too old; I have been Black for too long to love a white person that freely. Eventually life here takes everything from you.

I didn't know that I was headed toward Hollywood, but I soon realized I was. It occurred to me as I crossed the 710 on the 10 and I passed by my high school campus. I kept taking videos of myself as I drove. I wanted to fuck me, and it was a beautiful, powerful feeling. I wanted to share it with the world. I wanted to share it with the person in New York. I wanted to have her in the car next to me and tell her every story that I am telling you right now. I wanted to hear her silence as she listened to them. I wanted to hear her stories, every single one of them. Every boy she loved like she would never love again. Every person who said a casually racist thing to her that made her flinch and immediately shove the feelings down. I wanted her to fuck me. I wanted to fuck her. I wanted her to want to fuck her like I wanted to fuck myself. I wanted so much I thought I might erupt. I licked my lips, rubbed my hand on the gearshift, turned the music up. I felt like crying, but crying was too simple. But I did a little of it anyway.

My playlist landed on "In My Room," which I replayed again and again in the traffic on the 101. I'm too old to feel about Frank Ocean's music the way I do, it's just that he was one of the first Black men I'd ever heard who speaks the way my brain does—in hip-hop and queerness at the same time, in wordplays so pretty as to be lexical braggadocio unto themselves, in a cascading recounting of heartache and beauty, of violence described from the fleshy softness inside of it.

On Grindr I had a DM from someone named Marco. "Wow! You're Handsome" he began, capitalizing the first letter of every word. I thought this was odd since my face is largely obscured in my pics. His excitement, too, was slightly destabilizing. Grindr rules normally dictate that you speak mostly in the Courting Language of the Bros, in which you communicate a desire to devour someone without communicating any excitement about them. "Hey," "Sup," "Nice cock," "u suk?," and so forth. Marco was coming at me differently. I was inspired to let go of my own version of a Grindr performance to ask him how his evening was. "It's okay. I'm with my roommate but they're leaving soon," he responded before sending me a nude. I thought to ask if that was him or his roommate, but I wasn't sure the joke would land over DMs. The photo was mediocre, fuzzy through a cheap phone camera lens, taken from about chest to upper thigh, a body that looked simple, slightly aged. I got the sense that he wasn't a person with natural confidence, but rather an earned confidence.

Marco said he could host and told me he'd be back in a few minutes with an address. I waited. Soon he returned and told me to meet him at the gas station on the corner of Vine and Santa Monica. I was not sure why, but I presumed it had to do with safety. I was about five minutes away. I drove there, got out of the car, bought a pack of gum through the bulletproof window, and waited. Leaning on the hood, chewing. It was Saturday night in Hollywood. The anonymous free feeling that I sometimes get in Los Angeles was beginning to curl up around me from the ground, through my toes, taking my whole body in its twinkling grasp. The very first thing I loved about this city when I moved here in my teens was the fact that I could walk its boulevards alone, explore its crevices unbothered. I could have near-death experiences to which no one bore witness. For some reason I craved this then, found freedom in it. I still do.

After a while of watching the corner, I moved my car to the parking spots at the edge of the station and waited. Soon a slight Latinx man who looked to be in his late fifties wearing a stained button-up shirt and a pair of tearaway warm-up pants emerged on the sidewalk, checking his phone and then looking around. This had to be Marco. I watched him for a moment, and thought about watching him further, but this felt like an abuse of power, so I rolled down my window but said nothing. The movement attracted his attention. He smiled and nodded slightly and cased the immediate area before getting into my passenger seat.

As soon as he sat down, he reached over and rubbed his hand on my stomach, which I found incredibly bold. Like send me a random pic of your cock, sure, but don't touch my fat belly. "Wooooow," he said, looking at me admiringly. He had a thick accent. "You're so handsome!" I thanked him and returned the compliment, at first out of obligation, but it started to become clear that he was in fact handsome. He had a prodigious nose and warm, olive-black eyes. A day's worth of graying stubble lined his cheeks and thin wrinkles framed his eyes and mouth. His clothes were ill-fitting and slightly tattered. There was something both glowing and slightly fatigued about his entire countenance.

He admired me for a moment longer with his eyes lighting up. We began to kiss. His stubble was a lot. There was a not insignificant whiff of body odor. A part of me didn't want to kiss him and yet there was more of me that did. Anyway, it was too late because his tongue was already down my throat. I bent over so that I could get easier access to his cock, but the low bucket seats combined with the high center panel made it hard to get my mouth on it. Nonetheless he took it out. The word that came to mind was solid. It was a nice solid cock. Stable and sure of itself. Not garish or unusual in any capacity. A confident cock. A cock that would not start a fight but would be willing to stand up if someone vulnerable was being threatened. A cock with integrity. I tried to get it in my mouth.

An SUV pulled up next to us and even though it was 10:30 p.m. on a Friday, an entire family started piling out. Parents, grandparents, aunts and uncles, teens and toddlers. Marco hastily covered himself with the bottom of his button-up shirt and we decided that we should go elsewhere. He navigated me to a side street a few blocks away, where I parked behind a camper van.

He was a small man. It did not take a lot for him to

crawl over the seats and all over my body. He treated me like a cure for his hunger, devouring me, scratching me with his beard, whispering in Spanish in my ear. His smell was almost too much, but not quite. He was almost too much. There was a slight violence to the way he touched me, groped my neck, bit my cheek. This combined with a constant murmuring about how beautiful I was made me feel that I could be free with him. When he went down on me, a thing I was not expecting, I noticed that I did not feel self-conscious, self-aware. I was not afraid of what he would think, if he would be hurt, the way that I sometimes am with women. I was not worried about traumatizing him or retraumatizing him. I was not worried about the size of my cock. I felt safe fucking his face roughly. I was not ashamed of myself with him. I felt he understood the failures of men and forgave them.

I made it my mission to finish him off; I contorted my body over the center console and let him have his way with my mouth, losing myself in how he lost himself, his moaning, his pounding the roof of the car, the windows fogged beyond reason. He made a great deal of noise. He held me down. He fucked my face until he came loudly and prodigiously. I remained there for all of it. I rolled down the window and spit onto the street.

"Wow," he kept saying. "Wow-wee, wow!"

Driving back to where we had met, he had trouble reassembling his tearaway pants, which he had dramatically ripped off to facilitate the receiving of head. So, pantsless, he sat in the passenger seat while we got to know each other. He had to meet at a gas station because he thought his roommate was leaving but, in the end, surprise, he stayed. He liked his roommate, but he was sometimes very annoying and couldn't read social cues. He worked out at the gym in the mornings and loved yoga but unfortunately was nursing a shoulder injury. He's had a lot of fun on Grindr but not everyone is cool. Some men are terrible and mean and assholes. He wakes up early so he can journal. He's been in America for twenty years. He asked me if I was self-conscious when he touched my stomach. I helped him with the pants before answering. It was a lot of snaps.

"Yeah . . . a little . . . I mean I feel different on different days . . ." I began.

But I stopped because he was looking at me in a way that made me blink.

"Oh, baby . . ." he said, and reached out to stroke my cheek. "Baby, you should never change who you are just to make someone else happy. Because if you change one thing, then they just ask you to change something else, you know?"

"Yeah . . ." I said. Because I almost always say "yeah" when a man is telling me what to do, whether I mean it or not.

He looked at me and smiled as if he had just given birth to me.

"So beautiful."

I helped him get his pants situated. They are pretty complicated to manage in a car. Once he was finished, he opened the car door, put one foot out, and stopped. Looked back at me.

"Do you want to exchange numbers?"

I thought about it. I really did. The only reason I said no was because I realized in that moment that I was allowed to say no. Usually, I feel like I can't.

"No . . . I get to LA often. I'll find you on the app."

He looked disappointed. And I could tell he didn't believe me, which broke my heart a little. But he did not try to change my mind. This is how I knew his kindness was for real. I hate when I tell people no and they try to change my mind after I've said no. I hate it.

I did have every intention to find him on the app the next time I went to LA. But he either blocked me or made a new profile because next time I looked, our whole thread was gone from my DMs. Most of the people who messaged me that night were soon gone from my DMs.

Sex is weird and disgusting and ridiculous and quite often abused and weaponized and traumatic. But I still like it. I like what it can be and sometimes what it is. Sometimes I think it might hold the secrets to almost everything. If we can learn how to treat it with care, we may be able to heal every part of us that needs healing. Sometimes it's just nice to hold someone while they cum, kissing their earlobe and whispering to them *yes*. Sometimes it feels like that is the only important thing I was put here to do.

The Touch

Once, I was at a queer and trans POC sex party. It felt like the first time. I had been to other kink and sex events, but they were always overwhelmingly white. I used to think I was okay with that. I was young and I liked being an artist and exploring the world. Also, I wanted to die or destroy myself pretty much constantly. So maybe I wasn't as okay with that as I thought.

I have since tried to become a better person for myself. I have since tried to undertake the complete and complex work of becoming whole, trying to become at least some kind of version of the powerful human my mother and my ancestors might have wanted me to become, which meant trying as I might to detangle myself from whiteness in all its forms, both within and without me, and detangle myself from patriarchy and misogyny in all its forms both within and without me, and detangle myself from straight-ness in all its forms both within and without me.

After all that, I found it an exciting prospect to be in a room with all queer people, all non-white people, all sex-positive, kinky, perhaps nonmonogamous people, all of whom were trying to find their way, or cry their way, or fight their way, or cum their way to their own liberation and perhaps to my liberation, too; all people who knew that finding their way there meant being willing to genu-inely consider the upending of literally every system we had been taught to work in, every altar we had been taught to worship at; it meant being preached at and prayed over, dismissed and tossed aside by the families we had leaned on for love when we were very small; it meant being barred from group chats and family functions, bombarded with hate messages and DMs, attacked on the street for looking too different from the gender you were supposed to look like, posting stuff that gets you swarmed by white supremacists and Trumpers who send you death threats and call you faggot and nigger and monkey.

I wanted to be in a room of people whose liberation had taken them through that hell and who knew what it cost to be free and for whom that cost was not a choice or an option. I wanted to be with people who could not be alive unless they were free, not people who could be fine with a convenient amount of liberation because the world still generally worked for them no matter how many fucked-up systems were in place for everyone else. I didn't want to be with people for whom liberation was a vitamin, a nice thing that might enhance their lives and make things better and would be super cool and awesome if it came about. I wanted to be with people for whom liberation was a medicine, something without which they would simply die. That is why I went to the queer, trans, Black, Indigenous, POC sex party.

For safety reasons everyone had to arrive and leave with a buddy whose behavior they were responsible for and vice versa. Accordingly, I found myself embedded in a small group that consisted of a writer I had met about a year earlier through mutual friends and gone on one date with at a gay bar in Berkeley and a small assortment of people from the writer's life: a coworker of theirs, a downstairs neighbor, a teacher I would later learn was a poet. Everyone was dressed in glitter and feathers and bodysuits, lacy bralettes, and other finery. The poet was dressed in baggy jeans, a loose button-up shirt, a flatcap, like a substitute teacher who was popping by a family barbecue on the weekend.

The event began with an opening circle in which the organizers led everyone in a bunch of check-ins and woohoos and aren't we excited to be heres, which we all said we were. I was also nervous, but not about sex or the potentiality of it. I wasn't even sure if I was actually in the mood for sex because sex, as you know, is weird. I was just nervous because it was a party and I'm always nervous at parties. What if no one likes me? What if I'm alone and everyone else is happy? What if I'm seen and then rejected?

They talked us through the values of the space, why it was important to hold this gathering away from white people. I remembered then that when it was first proposed there had been a small dustup on the Facebook page, where one of the organizers had suggested that people should be able to bring their white partners and "allies." They were summarily dogpiled in the way superconscious people in this community dogpile, which was with well-thought-out arguments and lots of "I hear where you're coming from but what this brings up for me is . . ." Underneath the language what it really came down to was pretty much all Black women being like, "No. Like literally no. What the fuck?" The argument of course being that the whole point of this space was to be free and intimate away from whiteness and how can anyone do that if people won't even leave their white partners for a night?

Eventually the organizer admitted that they had not really thought this through and apologized. I watched the whole thing play out from afar, and with a not insignificant amount of internal cringe, I had to admit that I saw where he was coming from. I might have thought the same thing at some point in my life and that was embarrassing for me. One of the really neat tricks of oppressor systems is how they make you believe that you can be liberated from them while still deeply tied to them. I see why people want to believe that. It would be much easier for a lot of people if that were true. It's just that, well, it's not.

Throughout the opening circle, we cheered and snapped. There were lots of nods and heartfelt *mmmhm-mms* and *c'mon now*s. I got the sense that a lot of us spent a lot of our waking hours dealing with white spaces, personally, socially, politically, romantically. Tonight, therefore, had the feel of a family reunion, a small deliverance, of everyone getting a day off from the same grueling job at the same time. They role-played consent scenarios, conversations about boundaries and STDs. Onstage, one person asked another if they wanted to kiss. The second person said "no." The first person said, "Thank you for taking care of yourself." We all clapped.

I had never heard this before, thanking someone for saying no. It was an idea that made my brain twist around itself. I had always assumed that if you wanted to take care of someone else you said yes to whatever they asked. If you said no, you were disappointing them and abandoning them. Sometimes you might have to say no, but that was only for extreme circumstances. "No" was an act of aggression. "No" was an act of harm. I believed this so deeply that I didn't even know I believed it until I heard someone say that it was not true.

They also role-played conversations about what they were calling "aftercare," a term I had heard applied only to BDSM. I thought it was when you did intense pain or impact stuff with someone and then you held them afterward and told them it was all in good fun and that you didn't really think they were a worthless slut. But here they were talking about something else.

Role-Player 1: Would you be open to kissing and making out a little bit?

Role-Player 2: Why yes, I would!

Role-Player 1: Cool, great! And after we do that, what are you hoping our relationship will look like? Would you want to exchange numbers, get to know each other outside of here, or are you hoping that it's limited to this space?

Role-Player 2: Hmm, good question. I'm not sure, but for now I'm okay if we just limit it to this space, and if I feel differently later, can I let you know?

Role-Player 1: Yep. I'm also okay with limiting it to this space for now and then checking in later if we feel like that might change! Now let's fuck!

Everyone laughed and clapped. I was getting my mind blown. Who does this? Who talks about what they want and hope for before sex? Who says "no" so clearly? Who thanks someone they want to fuck for telling them "no," without it being part of some extended and passive-aggressive power play? No one had ever shown me that this was a possible way to interact with one another. I had the sudden feeling that the real secrets to life had been kept from me up until this very moment.

In an icebreaker we introduced ourselves to the people around us by telling them the mildest and wildest things we'd be happy to have happen for us tonight. It was a hard question for me. I've built an entire life on being okay with everything. How could I know what I wanted? The wildest thing was easy: to be lost in a writhing orgy of Black bodies, loving upon one another, kissing and fuck-

ing one another, creating a collective pleasure and freedom greater than any of us could find on our own. I didn't
even know if I wanted that. I just knew that's what I
thought I was supposed to want.

The question of mildest was much harder. What do
you want? What are you trying to get? What is important
to you? I was paired with a tall person in a thin black
dress, who towered over me, fixed me with a gentle, ex-
pectant look, glitter makeup around their eyes, a pearles-
cent shawl, a peacock-feather hairclip pin. They had
introduced themselves with a name that I now forget, but
I remember saying it back to them in that moment, briefly
thinking about how saying someone's name could be a
religious act.

I felt the heaviness and awkwardness of my body. I
was not tall, nor skinny, nor beautiful. I was a toddler
who barely knew how to walk or how to wrap my fingers
around a thing, and also I was an old and drooping man
who had seen too much wretchedness to be beautiful
anymore, if indeed he ever was. I tried to shake both feelings loose. I try to shake them loose even now as I recall
them.

I guess, I began, *the mildest thing I'd be okay with . . .*
They nodded slightly at me, their smile widening, their
blinking reminding me of the tiny threshing of butterfly
wings . . . *would be to meet someone who understands
how I feel?*

A beautiful Black burlesque dancer came out next
and performed for all of us, and it really did feel as

though he was doing it for us, offering up his body and his moves and his deepest, slowest, sexiest grinds for our salvation. And we were giving him the biggest love we could muster, probably because we knew that somewhere in his life someone had given him hate, someone had tried to destroy him for being in his body, as Black and as queer as it was, and it was as if we thought the concerted power of our cheers and cries, *oohs* and *aaahs*, our *yes lords* and *get its* could wipe him clean of the agony and loathing that had already been heaped on him and we wanted that so badly for him because we wanted it so badly for ourselves.

The party was declared underway. The DJ dropped a beat, people scattered with their collective groups, and the overwhelming feeling of loneliness returned. I talked a little here and there with the people I came with, but I was terrified to introduce myself to anyone or make any new friends, even though when I looked around, I saw people shaking hands and striking up conversations. I made sure my water bottle was filled, took frequent trips to the bathroom or the coat area, checked my phone a lot.

The Poet and I agreed that we would stick together so we wouldn't have to face the clumsiness of wandering around alone. The night wore on. A new DJ began. On the dance floor people flitted about, laughing, waving boas, entertaining each other. On the couches and beds upstairs, couples and groups made out, some people were fucking, others cuddling in piles. The Poet and I floated around like UN observers, talking about who we liked, who was pretty, whose vibe we admired, whose outfit we secretly coveted. Sometimes we were apart. I briefly made out with the writer who had brought the group together. It was goofy and ephemeral, but most of the time I didn't see her. Most of the time she was off having what seemed like a myriad of sexual experiences with other people. The music was better than I expected it to be.

We were on a couch near the dance floor. Not in the place where people were truly getting into it, which was upstairs, but downstairs in the more common shared area. Me, the Poet, the Writer. It was an hour or so until the party would be over. We were cuddling but it was mildly awkward. The Poet and I had developed a vibe that was sort of like when you're in elementary school at recess and you're a new kid and you feel hella weird, so you start hanging out with another weird kid on the playground and you don't know the kid very well but the main thing you like about them is the fact that they're hella weird like you, and you're just glad to have someone to hang out with while everyone else who won't talk to you is playing football or skipping rope. It was sort of like that for me with the Poet. We were awkward buddies. We clung to each other.

The Writer wandered off again and the Poet and I continued to wrap our arms around each other, slowly moving our hands up and down on each other's bodies. We now had some inside jokes, a one-word reference to something earlier in the evening, an agreeable silence. I was painfully aware of the back-and-forth movement of our hands on each other's skin, and it was like when you're fourteen at an amusement park and you're holding hands with someone you're supposed to be "going steady with" and you can't even enjoy it because all you can think about is if your hand is too clammy or if you're squeezing too tight. But also it felt nice to just be able to touch someone else's flesh for the simple reason that it did, and a human body is an amazing, magnificent thing, filled with cells and systems, throbbing arteries, soft flesh with little tiny hairs, and a heart that beats under it all trying and trying and trying every moment to keep us alive so we can love each other, and why wouldn't you want to lay your hand gently on the miracle of a body, to feel its heat and angles, its pulsing glow beneath your fingertips, if it was appropriate and safe to do so?

I asked them if they wanted to go upstairs. They pulled back and angled their head so they could look at me before saying a *yes* that was as small and sweet as a tiny drop of honey, barely audible over the music. We got up from the couch, walked to the stairs, climbed them together, and found a spot on a foam pad covered in clean faded floral sheets. On either side and all around us, people were fucking, moaning, cumming, holding one another in torrid embraces, letting themselves go, letting everything go.

We sat down facing each other and began to run our hands along each other's arms. I did not know how far we would go. I did not know how far I wanted to go or how far they did. *Would it be okay if we kissed*, one of us said. We did. *Would it be okay if I kissed your neck*, one of us said. They unbuttoned their shirt. We touched each other's bodies, cupped each other's faces in our two hands.

When your face is that close together with someone else's, there is a magic that happens. It is almost like they become a different person entirely, or rather everything you thought you knew about them—how they dressed, how they talked, where in the social order they fit—all of it disappears entirely, replaced by the wonder-working of intimacy. Another thing comes through, something clear, something simple and old, something that both is and isn't them. A spirit? An essence? I don't know. Maybe they just become a human in precisely the same way that you are human, without the tiniest shard of separation between you, and for a brief moment your forehead is pressed not against their forehead but against your own timeless nature, your lips are not against their lips but against the awakening, breathing possibility of their entire being. This happens only for an instant, though, a mere breath, barely a wink of time. It's the kind of thing where if you don't pay close attention, you might miss it entirely. That moment, I have come to believe, is another word for love.

Later I was home alone, trying to remember this event, to have it fossilized so that I could feel it forever and call upon it again and again. It was not working. I could not wrap my mind around it. I did not have an emotional language with which to understand what I had experienced. It was not sexual, even though it sort of looked like it was. It was something else entirely, though I don't exactly know what. I was lying in my bed trying to save this memory and failing and only then did it dawn on me how funny it was that this person and I were at a sex party, a literal orgy, like, full-on Babylon, like, the most X-rated shit ever, blow jobs, and cumming, and eating ass, and all manner of freaky-deaky shit happening within feet of us, and still we had taken three hours to progress to the point of holding hands.

We had taken each moment, each kiss, each caress, each unbuttoning with slowness, with care, with precision. I laughed and laughed, almost fell out of my bed.

This was the pace we found together. A pace that had to do with who we were in that moment and not what was expected of us, not how we were expected to feel or be because of where we were. We were moving, as adrienne maree brown says, at the speed of trust. I didn't want anything more than what we had, and I didn't want it to happen any faster than it did, because any more or any faster would not have been ours.

I have been taught, and perhaps you have been taught as well, that consent is a contract. You said this was allowed, so it is. This is what we agreed to, so this is what I'm owed. But there are many problems with this. It is transactional, treating sex as a market exchange rather than as a collaboration among humans. Also, it leaves too many possibilities for how something can be agreed to. Do you agree to do some horny shit because you've agreed to join me in a room full of people fucking? Did I agree to sex because we've been exchanging nudes and have spent a week saying nasty things to each other? Did we agree to the contract of fucking just because at one point we said or indicated we wanted to fuck?

Consent is not a contract or a promise. It is not an acceptance or an admission. It is a collaboration, an ongoing one. It is us, talking to each other over the course of the entire night, verbally, nonverbally, physically, spiritually, emotionally about what we each needed in place for the exchange between us to be fun and safe, willing and good. That is, in fact, exactly how they defined consent that night, in the opening circle. It's just that it took me three hours to learn with my body what that might mean.

I have struggled to explain this moment to my friends, lovers, to all of us who have been trained since the moment we could perceive the world in relationships and sex as another arena for ownership and exploitation, for getting what you want, for overcoming challenges and resistance. We are taught that if it is right, we will know what a partner wants without even having to ask. We are taught that the best sex comes when we are too overwhelmed with passion to resist it, that it must overtake all reason, all communication, and all care. We balk and shudder at the time it takes to find out who a person is and what they are comfortable with, what they need, what they are afraid of. We think that to spend this human time with a person, acknowledging who they are, should be reserved only for people we want to marry or partner with or otherwise acquire and bring into our lives and homes permanently. Sex is a deeply human act, perhaps the most human of all acts. So why are we taught to do it without acquiescing to the immutable fact of one another's humanity?

The following weekend a former friend with benefits came over to hang out. We had agreed several months prior that while we had a great time together, our sexual relationship had run its course and we should probably remain platonic friends. On my couch we watched television. She put her head on my lap. We began touching. Soon we were reenacting a sex scene from all the movies we had ever watched, ripping our clothes off, rushing to the bedroom. It was nice. It was fine. It was okay. It made my stomach hurt.

We did not check in about if this was a good idea; we hurried through an incomplete agreement about safe sex. Some tiny part of me was asking to be heard, telling me that we didn't have to actually have sex right then, was not even sure if we wanted that. We could breathe and stop and make sure that we were both fully okay with what was about to happen. Or we could talk about what might be keeping us from being fully on board, lightly, lovingly, cracking jokes, holding hands. Listening to each other.

But there was more of me that was afraid of "ruining the vibe," or worse, making her feel like I didn't want her badly enough. I realized in that moment, as everything was tumbling out of my grasp and back into the clutches of what it has been for my entire life, that this was the kind of sex I had always had; sex as the result of a kind of momentum, sex under a threat, a threat that if I said no, then someone would be hurt, a fear that if someone was hurt, then I'd be hurt. Sex as an obligation.

I remember when I would sext with someone for weeks, sending pics and making plans to come to their place on Friday or Saturday night. But when the day would come, I would start to get the same feeling of dread in my stomach that I had when a kid said they were going to beat me up after school. I never knew what to make of that feeling. Shouldn't I push past it? Isn't it unmanly to miss out on getting some because of a little case of the butterflies? What if I say no tonight and no one ever offers to have sex with me again? How are you supposed to be a man and be ambivalent about sex, or to have any relationship with it that was more complicated than "always trying to get some"? That is not a rhetorical question. I am genuinely asking. Who can I look to to show me how to do that, how to be that? Who has ever shown me?

So much of my life begs of me not to be human, not to feel things too deeply, not to care too much, hesitate too much, desire too much, not to say what it feels like, not to admit that I am broken or afraid or overstimulated or hurt or lonely or unsure, not to admit that I need and want and hope and dream. This is what we as men are taught everywhere. This is what I learned about sex. Men are trained to be sexual automatons—beings with one drive that we execute faithfully under all conditions without regard for any of the confusions, complexities, softnesses, twists and turns, doubts and longings of our humanity or anyone else's. And because we are trained to view ourselves as sexual automatons, when these confusions and complexities arise, we shove them down. They do not match our programming and in the moment we have no way to resolve that contradiction. Instead we aim our will toward the acquisition of sex like we are completing a spiritual purpose. And when someone stands in the way of that spiritual purpose, we become disillusioned and angry and accusatory. We do not learn how to be human beings in connection with ourselves; we learn only to get our feeling of being alive by taking something from another person, by owning them, occupying them. Colonizing them. And so, we cannot hear our "no's." There is no room for the "no" inside of us. And if we cannot hear our own "no's," if we cannot understand our own ambivalence, if we do not know how to listen with precision, and delicacy and susceptibility to the whispers of our bodies and hearts and souls, then how can we ever, even for a moment, listen to anybody else's?

The No

When I was growing up the word "consent" was barely a part of any language spoken by me or anyone I knew. In 1995, I was in my early twenties and "rape" was a word tossed around often, and it meant when someone attacked you. What happened to me when I was seven in the downstairs bathroom with the razor blades wasn't rape as far as I knew because I was a kid, and it was my fault and I let them do what they did to me because I wasn't tough enough and I couldn't fight. The very first rule of boyhood is you have to know how to fight, and if you can't fight then anything that happens to you is your fault because you should have known how to fight.

What happened to me when I was eight with my babysitter wasn't rape as far as I knew because I had kind of liked it and female nakedness is a commodity and a thing you're supposed to be acquiring and I had gotten some. How can the acquisition of something that you're supposed to be acquiring count as a harm against you? It can't. I didn't understand this when I was in my early twenties, new to adulthood and manhood. I thought only that I had been likable enough that a babysitter let me play with her breasts. This was an accomplishment. I thought that my rapes happened either because I was too weak to stop them or because I was good enough to earn them.

Once, in 1995, in my twenties, I was sharing a bed with an ex, and we had been sleeping together intermittently even after we broke up. That night, I tried to talk her into sex. She did not want to, but I kept insisting, pleading my case. We were kissing a little bit and making out, and I put my hand between her legs and felt that she was wet. I thought this meant that even though her mouth was saying no, her body was saying yes.

This idea didn't come from nowhere. In that precise moment a scene flashed in my head from an old television show I had watched when I was a kid in which a woman was on a date and the guy was chasing her around the couch, "getting fresh," as it might have been referred to in the parlance of the show. The whole bit was played for laughs. He chased, she ran, they stopped and delivered punch lines. My brain latched on to the scene. It lodged itself in my memories for the rest of my life, and for no apparent reason. I remember thinking once when I was in theater school about the choreography that must have gone into that scene, how many times they had to rehearse

it to get it right. I knew how hard it was getting the co-
medic timing on a thing like that, but these were profes-
sionals. It had worked, the audience was rolling. "Your
mouth says no but your eyes say yes!" he said breathlessly
before launching in pursuit of her once more. The studio
audience screamed. It was one of those seventies sitcom
moments where the audience *is* the show, they're all over
themselves, falling out of the chairs, you're laughing at
home, we're all having a shared moment of joy. What an
event. *I am not alone. I love this show.*

I remember thinking of this in the moment with my
college ex, how he had said, "Your mouth says no but
your eyes say yes." That line had never made sense to me,
which is why I remembered it from my childhood in the
first place, but in that moment, I finally understood it.
This was what was happening with the person in front of
me. Her mouth was saying she didn't want to, but her
body was saying she did. I was attractive enough that
even when she didn't want to have sex with me, her body
couldn't resist. I was good enough to earn it. I was able to
convince her.

Afterward she said: "I'm disappointed in you." I asked
why. I did not know. She said, "I never thought you were
the kind of person to do something like that." I asked what
she meant. She said, "I said no. And you kept pushing."

Why was it only then that I realized her "no" had
meant "no"? Not "no but yes," but simply "no."

Why was it only then that I realized that?

I apologized. I was ashamed. I could not find words
that expressed how sorry I was.

Why was it that I had assumed her body was an invitation?

I was shocked.

Why was I shocked?

I simply could not find the words.

I still have not found them.

That is because there are no words that can match what it means to put a millennium of violence onto the body of someone who took the risk of loving you.

Years later, after we were both married and we were both parents, we talked over email. I apologized again for it; she apologized for other things that happened in our relationship. She said something about us both being young.

Her forgiveness was a relief. Her forgiveness made me feel sick.

I met up with her a little while later, I met her kids, shook hands with her husband, we hugged under a tree in Berkeley. She DMed me about maybe moving back to the Bay and told me to keep my eyes open for places and I told her I would. That was a few years ago. We have drifted apart. We still occasionally like each other's posts but she's not super on social media these days. She lives in nature.

The thing about a moment like this is that it never ends. Our entire lives are shaped by it. After I got sober I found myself thinking of it every day, discovering new feelings about it, now grief, now deep shame, now anger at myself, now rugged determination to do everything I can to make sure that the part of me that was capable of doing this—the part of me that did do it—is never, ever in charge of anything in my life ever again, now struggling with how to forgive myself, now hopeless about how bad it all is, how unfixable this male violence all seems, now determined to heal every man I know from it, and to heal every woman who needed every man to have been healed many, many years ago, now just accepting. Now accepting of it all. I am not safe. You are not safe. We are just trying to be.

Someone once told me that there is no such thing as apology, there are only amends, and to amend something doesn't mean to change it, it means to add to the record. You can never erase the record. What you can add to the record is new behavior. The old behavior is an entire lifetime of indoctrination. The new behavior is an entire lifetime of practice.

I used to tell my children when they were little that what we do matters more than what we think or feel because what we do can never be changed. Attitudes can be changed, thoughts can be changed, but actions never can be. They are permanently etched into our lives and the lives of the people we impact. Every single time I said that, I was thinking of that moment in my bed in 1995. This is why people don't understand how to apologize. Because the same culture that taught me that "your mouth says no but your eyes say yes" was a punch line also taught me that an apology should be able to make an action disappear, as if you could delete a file on someone else's hard drive. When you hurt someone, you cannot unhurt them.

This is where people become angry and dismissive

and violent. Many of us do not like the idea that we cannot undo what we have been trained to do, that we cannot buy freedom from ourselves no matter how much money or effort or emotional output we spend. This goes against our training. We are trained as capitalists, just as we are trained as colonizers, and we are trained as rapists. Even when we are the colonized, even when we are the assaulted. We are trained to believe that with enough work, or sacrifice, or effort, or power we can acquire whatever it is that we want. Naked women. Money. Forgiveness. Freedom. Happiness. Innocence. Value. Worth. Land. Serenity. Hope. Absolution. We are trained that emotional and spiritual growth is merely the act of acquisition. *What are you going to do*, a Black meditation teacher once said with a kind smile as she rested the infinity of her eyes on me, *sit on this cushion and ride your way to freedom?*

I can never be free of what happened that night in my bedroom. Why should I be? This is not "beating myself up" or "lacking self-forgiveness." This is called genuinely caring about what you do, who you are, and what impact you have on people. As a man I am taught that I should never fall prey to the trap of genuinely caring. To experience discomfort for the sake of a woman is to be a simp, which is not to be a real man. Manhood, as we learn it, is predicated on making other people feel the discomfort that you should be feeling. Men tell themselves and one another that we must be free at all costs, and we are willing to earn our freedom on the backs of the people who we make suffer and the people who we hurt. If you are a man, if you have hurt a woman, and you most definitely have, I want you to lean in very closely and listen very carefully to the following words:

You can never be free. Apology is not enough. Healing is not enough. Time is not enough. What you can do is never enough because what you have done is bigger than you will ever be.

The closest you may come is to turn yourself over and over and over again to the honest, divine, and wholly annihilating practice of love.

The Love

Did you know that love is meant to be liberation?
Yes, I forget that sometimes too. Did you know that
love lives in the body? Yes, this I also forget. Did you
know that love is beyond language, even though we are
forever trying to find language for it? It sounds like a contradiction, but it is not. The language is an offering. A
symbol. A gesture, not unlike what a mortal would make
to a god. My little handfuls of marigolds and honey, incense and agua de florida cannot reach the heavens any
more than my words can reach to the center of our love.
The heavens, like our love, are everything and nothing;
the heavens, like our love, are everywhere and entirely
unseen. Still, it is nice that we try. It's nice that we brought
with us an orange, laid it down reverently at the feet of
the statue, bowed our heads, and felt—or imagined we

felt—a presence, and allowed that presence to grow within us. It is nice that we cast aside for a moment everything that was not that presence, devoted ourselves only to that presence, and that we do it every morning or evening, through rains and winds, for no reason other than to make an offering.

If the gods are pleased by any aspect of human worship, I would have to think that it is not by our oranges, or our incense, or even our magnificent wreaths, but rather by our striving. Our earnestness. The attempts of our hearts to reach the winds and be felt by the cosmos, all the while knowing full well those hearts are trapped inside bone cages and forever glued to the earth.

I heard once that the part of our brains that lights up when we see puppies trying to do things like climb stairs or play with a ball is the same part of an elephant's brain that lights up when they see humans. In other words, elephants think it's cute how we run around doing stuff just like we think it's cute when puppies do the same. As luck would have it, I recently found myself at a group luncheon with the head of a large zoo famous for its elephant enclosure and I asked her about this. "Hm. I haven't heard that," she said, shoving a samosa in her mouth, "but I doubt it. Humans are much more obnoxious than puppies."

Speaking of obnoxious, I also heard that the jazz composer Charles Mingus would write notes for instruments that were outside of the instrument's range. So, for the tenor sax, let's say—which at concert pitch goes from Ab2 to E5—he might write a melody with an F#5 in it.

When the tenor players in his orchestra would read the charts and point out that there was no way they could play the note as written, Mingus would reply: "I know that. But the sound of you trying is what I'm going for."

This is what words are to me. The sound of us trying.

Someone told me recently that the purpose of exercise is to experience the pleasure of your body. I don't know why I hadn't thought of that before. I knew that this was one of the purposes of sex. I knew that this was a purpose of eating, and dancing, and lying on a blanket in the sun in a park on a weekend afternoon, nodding in and out of sleep while a small party of people twenty feet over from you laugh and play music, but it did not occur to me that experiencing pleasure is a thing that could be done during exercise.

Recently at the gym, I focused on this—pleasure— and the result was subtle and profound. Everything moved more slowly, more clearly. The weight training felt almost . . . sensual? There was none of the mild but unmistakable panic I experience when I'm moving heavy plates with large muscle groups. It was as if, for the tiniest moment, my body actually belonged to me. It was not a broken, heavy thing that my brain drags up and down the stairs like so much luggage. For a moment it was my brain itself. It was my heart and my music and my whole consciousness.

I also found that I could focus more easily, experience less distraction from the gym characters who usually annoy me—loud grunting guy, the bros group who performs such stock characters of masculinity for one another that I wonder if they don't rehearse beforehand. At some point during all this, probably between the fourth and fifth deadlift sets, I thought of love. Or maybe it's more accurate to say I *felt* of love. I found it there riding the wave of light between my tendons, spreading across the broad wave of my shoulders, returning me to you over and over again. I felt of love and it was warm and kind and perhaps infinite. But only for a moment. For the rest of the day I walked around feeling in touch with an ease and power running through my body that I was not used to feeling. But then I lost it. Isn't that funny?

I don't know how love is supposed to be liberating when it lies trapped within us, when there is no amount of talking or writing or holding or fighting or kissing or fucking or conscious uncoupling that can ever hold it all. I find myself returning once again to an idea that keeps haunting me: love often feels less like freedom from struggle and more like struggle for freedom, an impossible and intermittently sublime attempt at deliverance that we knowingly submit ourselves to again and again. Maybe that's the liberation: waking up every day with absolute certainty of what our devotion will be. Maybe the liberation is in waking up every day and knowing we are longing for a thing that we will never be finished seeking.

Once, I went into a sauna and decided I would stay there until I saw god. It was 190 degrees, 12 percent humidity.

I didn't want to die, I just wanted to break for a moment from the surly bonds of the day. The confusion and fear, fatigue at work, competing deadlines, money owed, heartbreaks and vulnerabilities with loved ones, anger and weariness at the world, at our murders and our destructions, at our lies and our bullshit discourses, at our performances and our collective inability to overcome our collective weakness.

I had cried all week, but I had not told anyone about it because everyone I knew was crying louder and needed more love. I had tried to love people into freedom, I had tried to love myself into freedom. I had failed. My body bore the scars of it. There were aches and tremors, slivers of lightning in my joints, tears in my fabric, holes in my cloth. A writing student asked me to send them my favorite texts about love for a piece they were working on. I promised I would, but for some unknown reason I burst into tears the moment they left the classroom. It was a reasonable response. My pieces were disengaging from their center.

In the sauna I hoped not to come back together but to complete the disengagement. If I'm going to fall apart, let me fall all the way apart. All the way to god and all the way to the earth and to you. My body was covered in sweat. I felt it on my thighs, caressed it into the curve of my belly. I opened myself all the way up to anything and everything the world had for me.

My body has kept me alive, in spite of everything. In spite of how it has been robbed and violated and broken open, how it has been looted and ripped apart, sometimes by others and sometimes by me. I have driven my body into moving buses, and onto city asphalt with a bicycle under me and the wheels of a cab looming over my head. I have given myself concussions and fractures and bloody knuckles and bleeding wrists. I have drowned my body in whisky, buried it in cocaine, tried to dissolve it in columns of smoke, using my lungs like kindling to heat a fire that would maybe keep me warm during the long, cold nights.

My body has kept me alive, in spite of everything.

My body has made me a target, and an enemy. It has called the police to me, weapons drawn, as surely as if I had dialed the phone myself. It has made people afraid of me. It has advertised to other men that I mean to threaten them, challenge their dominion over the tiny spot of earth to which they have foolishly tried to lay claim. My body has invited them to push up on me, ask me where I was from, rain down blows and kicks on me, spit on me, leave me bleeding. My body has fought for itself and maybe for you. It has wrestled its way out of headlocks and leg locks and ground and pounds. My body has been the only thing between your feet and the concrete.

My body has shut down, pulled the curtains, locked the doors, sealed the windows. My body has closed up shop, leaving me to sit in darkness and silence, alone and cold.

In the sauna I wanted to move but even the towel was too hot in the places where I wasn't sitting on it. So, I breathed slowly, marveling at the miracle of breath. No one tells me to breathe, no one shows me how, and yet my body has done it every day, over and over and over again, no matter what.

My eyes were closed. I was clinging to the cooling wind of my breath. It was all I had. The heat was pulling me apart, pulling myself out of me.

I wondered if that's not what liberation is sometimes—the pulling of myself out of me, the opening of my body to receive all that my ego and my fear and my brain cannot hold on their own. The emptying of myself.

My body held my daughter's and my son's bodies the very moments they were born. My body held them for years and they were maybe the sweetest and best years of my life, though at the time they were the worst and most unwieldy and exhausting years of my life—having two toddlers fumbling around, spilling things, throwing tantrums, throwing toys, throwing up, and demanding milk three degrees hotter or four degrees cooler than I had made it. Ziploc bags and Cheerios and diapers and binkies and stuffies and car seats and strollers and swings and snacks and enough smushed bananas to wallpaper the US Capitol building. Those were the worst years of my life at the time and are the best years of my life now, because my body had a very simple purpose, and it was to care for them and their bodies.

How I loved having them to care for. How imperfectly I did it, how beautifully I did it, beautifully enough that they don't need me to care for their bodies anymore. They now have hair in strange places, and they smell funny and have zits at the ends of their noses that they pick at obsessively until they burst in a fountain of pus that they have to hide with toilet paper during second-period AP US history.

I was sweating my tears out. I was sweating all of it out.

The point of a body. What is it?

It is to survive. To love. To please. To fight. To hold me as I move through this world, to deliver my love to you. And to you. And to you. And to you. And to me. And to you. That is the point of my body. To deliver love.

I don't know if I found god in the sauna. It may have been in the cold plunge after. I mean cold. Ice-cold. Okay, it was 50 degrees, which is not ice-cold but feels ice-cold after 190 degrees and 12 percent humidity. I walked down the steps into the pool, my legs dissipated beneath me. It felt at first as though small knives were poking my thighs, and then it felt like nothing was touching me at all. I knew that this is the moment in which a decision must be made. Either you get out or go all the way in. Most of me wanted to get out. It was too cold. I was too afraid.

But there was a small part of me that knew my whole life lived right there below the surface of this water because my whole life comes down to a willingness to feel. *To feel.* Everything. Pain and fear. Love and cold. Nothing and all. I want to feel you hurting, I want to feel your anger. I want to feel your touch on the small of my back. I want to feel your distance, your history, your aches and pains and traumas. It is sometimes overwhelming and frightening. I may struggle to hold it. But still, I want it. That is what my body is for. To feel. In an instant, I went below the water and the cold covered all my sins, broke all my shells, turned me into nothing. To feel everything. To become nothing. Taken together, these two, perhaps, are love.

When I was seven years old, my uncle taught me how to swim in the YMCA pool. I had been terribly afraid of the water then. But I was gently held by a man who would later throw me across furniture. I was shivering and small, wet and panicked. Flailing about in the expanse of a pool so infinitely and unrelentingly neon blue. His arms, it seemed, were the only thing keeping me alive.

The Mother

When my kids were little, I co-led a baby and par-
ent sing-along. My son was in preschool, but my daughter was young enough to sit on my lap while we sang
about how the ocean refuses no river and how we loved
the flowers and the daffodils. I sang. The mothers sang.
The babies did not sing but they seemed happy enough.
My daughter wore pink overalls, and her arms were so
chubby that every single person who saw her made a joke
about eating her. It was Los Angeles in the mid-2000s.
Most parents in that room had tried, at some point, to be
famous and/or rich. Most had not succeeded. And yet
here we were, babies in arms, sitting on the floor of the
American Legion Hall singing songs that sometimes
would make us cry. We were performers performing true
feelings with no one watching but our toddlers.

I've been thinking about loving the daffodils a lot lately. I think I really do love them. They are funny. Small and perfect. Devoid of chaos. A star flower. A parking lot flower. A self-contained celestial fragment flower. I saw some when I went for a walk with my love in the Maryland suburbs where we were staying as I visited family. The older generation, my mother's siblings—many of whom had a hand in raising me—are collectively experiencing the effects of aging. One aunt had a stroke, an uncle with cancer, another aunt on an oxygen tank. "We're just going to start dying one after the other, one after the other," my aunt Annalee blurted out to me when I went to visit her.

We were looking over old photographs at the time. She was quietly remembering who each person was, what it was like that summer they had the cookout on Manor Avenue, describing the methods they used to keep their afros so powerful and perfect. There were long pauses between her sentences. When I first got there, she told me the stroke she had a few weeks earlier was the first time in her life she had felt "old." And yet there she was, minutes later, saying that they were all going to start dying one by one. I remembered in that moment that life comes at you fast even if it takes an entire lifetime to do it.

The daffodils are interesting because they don't seem to grow in huge clumps, nor do they look as though they were landscaped into being in the way the rest of the suburban flowers look. Most of the flowers there were in neat rows or perfect circles surrounding acacia trees, their colors popping off like fireworks preserved against a background of night-black mulch. The daffodils, by contrast, were just there. No plan, no accompaniment. It is not right to say that they grow "wild" because it is rare for daffodils to grow from seed. It is more likely that someone somewhere in an unspecified past planted two or three bulbs along the side of the road and now they bloom every year. They are perennials, members of the amaryllis family. Even when they don't appear to be, daffodils in this region are almost always the sign of human activity. There are stories about them blooming of their own accord in wild natural areas only for it to be revealed that an entire house had been there before. Whenever you see a clump of daffodils standing alone in a field, it is a sign that someone once tried to make something beautiful there.

My aunt seems to forget that she is aging. I was going to help her move a piece of furniture and instead of showing me where it was, she began trying to pull it out from the back of the closet herself. For the first few seconds I thought she was making some kind of joke, so absurd to me was the idea that she might be lifting a piece of furniture. She was not. I playfully chided her and moved it myself. It was slightly heavy, not insanely so. But the moment stuck with me and kept replaying in my mind.

When I was little, she took care of me while my mother went away to go to school. In my earliest memories she is making me Cream of Wheat, managing a household with a husband, a daughter, and me—a nephew/son. In my earliest memories, she is quiet, observant, stalwart, sharp, elegant, trustworthy. Gentle. A wry wit, an explosive laugh, a cigarette between thin fingers, smoky topaz skin that gleamed bronze in the sunlight. She once made an outfit that won her $500 at an Earth, Wind & Fire contest. She once gave me money to buy a keyboard when I inexplicably thought I was going to be a professional keyboardist. She ran a community mentoring program at the US Treasury. She showed me how to make macaroni and cheese. She called me every time my name popped up on TV or in the newspaper. My mother moved away from her siblings when I was little, and as a result, I grew up away from them. I started a life in California, three thousand miles away from her. My kids are there, my job is there, much of my life is there. And it is only now occurring to me what this truly means.

When I finally said goodbye to her at the end of my visit, I held her in my arms and told her how much she meant to me. The top of her head barely reached the crook of my neck. I felt a tiny tremble in her body, which I suppose surprised me a little but should not have. I made some joke like "Let's not get emotional, now," and she laughed. But I don't know why I made that joke. We should have gotten emotional. Emotions are how we communicate love, connection, care. Emotions are how we remind each other and ourselves that we are more than thoughts, more than money, more than plans or accomplishments or savings or jobs. Emotions are how we remember that we are only along for the ride.

When I was looking at the daffodils, it occurred to me that the beauty is much the same as emotions. It is nonsensical and it has no use but to remind us that there is more than us. I might call that "more than us" god but I know that you might not.

Everyone grows up and grows old. Everything changes. My daughter drives now and plays lacrosse and is planning road trips to visit colleges. I still love the flowers and the daffodils. I still have the feeling of holding a woman who raised me in my arms. I guess it's all going to be evidence that someone once tried to make something beautiful here.

As my love and I walked we noticed a rustling in the bush and I remembered that it was early spring, a time that is supposed to be related to resurrection. We don't do resurrection quite the same way back in California because nothing ever dies there, and time is not a circle. There it is more like a dot, a singular point at which all things, past and future, perpetually coexist. But I grew up on the East Coast, which is where I am now. Here, things go away and return. Trees, fruits, birds, plants, flowers, even the light disappears, dying right before your eyes only to emerge once again like a perpetual magic trick that nature has been performing for a million seasons.

The rustling was a bird, an American robin, its red breast thumping, nosing its way through the low branches dotted with scattered buds. It was our second time around the lake on our walk. I stopped to look at the bird and also to catch my breath. My walking partner seemed less interested in the bird than I was, which is understandable. The American robin is not remarkable, it is basic. Despite being one of the most common birds in North America, it still contains the power to fascinate me. Gray-black plumage with a bold, rust-colored breast, intense white-ringed eyes, and pale trims on its feathers that curve like a song whispered to the wind. How can an entire life exist in a body so small? How can something so common be so exquisite? That right there is nature's wildest poetic trick.

My aunt Leora is one of the three remaining who are still living in the area. She was the one who kicked us out in the snow, that night so many Februarys ago. Despite this, in my childhood, I remember her as unspeakably gorgeous and elegant. She drove a gold 1972 Pontiac LeMans, which seemed to me the most regal vehicle a person could have; more than a car—a Chariot of the Golden Diva in my mind, with white seats as wide as an ocean. It rode like it was being carried by the current.

In my memory she was all shimmering earrings and floral polyester, a body that looked the way a hug feels, a laugh that echoed from the wood-paneled rec room walls and held us in its arms the same way the albums on the stereo held our hips and made them dance. Bobbi Humphrey, Teddy Pendergrass, Sister Sledge, Stephanie Mills, Patti LaBelle, Donna Summer, Barry White. My aunt got down. We all got down.

Now it is many years later. I am in my late forties, so old that I must stop and look at birds as an excuse to catch my breath. Her life is largely confined to a bed and the easy chair that sits next to it. She still smokes. Her voice is still a song, just in a different key. Each sentence still a pronouncement. She still laughs like she is shaking fruit from a tree. When I was a teenager, I thought you could pull things over on her because she drank a lot. Now it seems as though she is incapable of missing anything. Maybe she always was.

Talking with her is like playing a video game where the boss attacks you slowly enough that you think you should be able to dodge the blows, but you somehow never can. I interviewed her once for a book project that has not materialized in the way I thought it would and the thing that struck me most was her power as a human being. Whether that power was for something you liked or something you did not like didn't matter. She seemed to be coming from a source much deeper in the earth than many of us, or maybe much closer to the sun. It was as if the ancestors liked her voice and chose to use her in order to be heard. It was not the words that mattered, of course. It was the music of her voice that seemed to carry them.

Spring means renewal, which means change. It means that things are born, which means that things die. The robin is supposed to be the first sign of spring because it is among the first to return from its vast annual tour of the earth. These little, tiny birds, usually weighing no more than three ounces, fly up to 250 miles every day during migration. Though their home is the United States, vagrants from the migration pattern have twice been recorded as far away as England. This means that at least twice a bird weighing three ounces has flown alone across the entire Atlantic Ocean just so that it might sing its music for different ears. Lately I have been imagining this journey. The days and nights, the vast darkness of the ocean, an endless sky, the hushed certainty. A force that knows only to go until it cannot go any more. What is life other than the irrepressible drive to do this?

It has become something of a quiet family joke that my aunt Leora is, in some sense, indestructible. I suspect this has to do with how hard she seemed to live at times—cigarettes and alcohol—not to mention how hard it felt at times to live with her because hard living is not a thing that can be done without affecting the people around you. She has been on and off oxygen and has limited mobility for years. But she continues unbowed. The ancestors are not done speaking through her yet, I suppose. The last time I saw her she told me that her advice to her granddaughter was not to pay attention to men's words because men lie. We both laughed, but I'm not sure we were laughing for the same reasons. With that said, maybe you should disregard everything I've written here. Everything I know about anyone, I know only from a distance.

A funny thing about American robins is that they get drunk. They will flock together, gorge themselves on fermented berries from the pyracantha bush, one of the few berries available during winter, and if they eat enough of them they will start to stumble around and fall over while walking. What better way to celebrate the miracle of having both a life and a death, a disappearance and a return? To be able to fly forever, and then to drink of god's fruit so hungrily, so voraciously, that you are not even able to walk?

We continued to walk. I want to say it was unseasonably cold, but what are seasons now anyway, other than a memory of a time in which we thought the world would move according to our expectations? Just the day before, there had been hail. Now tiny flecks of snow danced in the sky. There was a vastness to the fields and trees, a heaviness to the cold. It reminded me of frozen ground, which in turn reminded me of times in which people sometimes walked this Maryland soil with bare feet, a thing I always think about when I'm in this part of the country. Slavery hovers over my mind here like an intrusive thought. The county I was in had at one time been the biggest slave-owning region in the state of Maryland. We were walking on land that had once been a part of an empire lorded over by Oden Bowie, the thirty-fourth governor of the state of Maryland. If you were in the buying mood, his plantation home half a mile away from where we strolled could be had for a little over $1 million.

The sky expands in a place like this. The vast strip malls and semi-gated communities are no match for it. Neither are the trees, which all seem to stop growing at the same height as if under a collective agreement not to get too tall. Sometimes you'll be driving one of these country routes and the roadside trees will give way to a field or farm that seems to extend as far as you can see.

Coming from California, where I can—in a single day—experience sixty-foot ocean waves and trees taller than the US Capitol building, I tend to think of Maryland as small by contrast—compact, cozy, intimate. But these vistas betray a vastness that always surprises me even though I've been seeing them my whole life.

We had found a tiny lake and we were walking around it. The wind battered our faces, and we tilted our heads downward against the cold. We had been talking about family and birds, beignets and sororities. What we were not talking about is what was on my mind: my uncle, who I had seen a day earlier. His face haunted me in the silences between us.

His hair had been snow-white, as was his beard. It was the first time in my entire life that I had seen him like that. It reminded me of the time when I was six years old and he dressed up as Santa Claus. I knew it was him, but I also knew it was Santa. Both things could be true. Funny how that works. Now, even in his midseventies, and even after a round of chemo, he still had a mostly full head of hair, a fact in which I found myself taking an absurd comfort, being that he is the closest glimpse I have into my own genetic future. We not only have the same genetics, we also have the same name. This meant that when I surveyed his dining room table, which was filled with what looked like literally a hundred prescription bottles, all I saw was my name on them over and over and over. The image hit me so hard and so immediately that I filed it away and didn't think of it again until I tried to sleep later that night.

He had understandably lost weight, his shoulders were thin, his bathrobe hanging on them as though they were exposed steel beams. His posture was hunched. He sat down, propped himself up over the table on one elbow while he leaned to the side like an ancient tower. He had raised me. He had slammed me against walls when my homework wasn't good enough. He had shown me how to throw a football, use a circular saw, give a decent handshake. He had told me every day that I could be great if I wanted to. He once bought me a leather portfolio to organize my work and inside he had written the phrase "organization is the key to success." I was in third grade. He taught me how to do electrical wiring when I was twelve. He was a master electrician. He took pride in it. He mentored young apprentices with the same love and guidance with which he mentored me. He was one of the world's greatest mansplainers, truly exquisite at the craft. He brought me with him to the community college course he was taking because he wanted me to be around smart people. Afterward he helped me think through the problems they had discussed in his logic class. He took me on errands, answered all my questions about life and the world, memories, time, history, the military, food, science. He took it upon himself to make sure I understood the world. He made me feel, at times, smart and valuable.

He was like a father to me with everything that means. And one of the things that means is that he looms so large in my memory and my imagination that every day of my adult life, I now realize, I am confronting some ghost of him.

The lake was small, cold, and clear. I found myself drawn to it, wanting to circle it again and again. It seemed to hold something I needed but I did not know what it was. It just felt like peace. I just liked how the water reflected the sky, how the graying winter light muffled the trees around it, which were all bare, save for the occasional cherry blossom. The whiteness of his hair. It was like snow. It was like glass.

I liked the irritated geese who slowly moved out of our way each time we passed them on the path. *Jesus fucking Christ, you again??* they seemed to be saying with their recalcitrant waddle. I liked our heavy breathing as we wordlessly pushed the pace of our steps, the sweat and heat forming under my black turtleneck. It seemed a miracle that I could walk, a miracle that I could generate my own heat. Indeed, it was. Each normal breath I took—of which I had taken millions and of which I naively expected to take millions more—was a miracle.

What had struck me most about my uncle when I saw him for the first time after his diagnosis was not his frailty but his beauty. The clarity in his eyes, the purity in his voice. It was not an aesthetic beauty but an ordinary human one. A miraculous one. "One thing that's changed," he said through a voice driven gravelly with time and radiation, "is I can't stand the bullshit anymore. I just don't have the capacity for it."

Here his eyes were like the lake: Clear, reflective, still. Of unknown depth. Untroubled. To see a person who has troubled you for years in that state is a miracle unto itself.

It rained off and on when I drove back from visiting him. Patches of clouds gave way to narrow beams of majestic sunlight that looked like stock photography on a Christian greeting card. Passing by a row of electrical transmission towers I noticed that a singular ray of sun was lighting up the ceramic insulators, turning them into sticks of white neon, radiating foolishly bright against the afternoon sky. I did not know what I was seeing, I just knew that it was beautiful. Within seconds, however, my position had changed and the glowing light was gone. They were just boring old electrical wires now.

I remembered the whiteness of his hair and beard, how it had suited him, turned him into someone both strong and angelic. Maybe that was just an optical illusion too. I am reminded that the less we can hide, the more beautiful we are. Maybe that's why I like weather like this. It is cold. But it is clear.

The way I love cherry blossoms has always, to me, felt kind of weird. More than just being unmanly, I've been concerned by how basic it is to love these trees that bloom every spring in DC and to which so many people come to visit that they have to reroute traffic along the main boulevards. How can a love be real if the object of it is so generic?

They grow around my California home, too, a thing I first started noticing a few weeks after I had my heart broken so badly that I suffered from panic attacks for months after it happened. My heart wasn't broken because I loved the person so; rather, it was broken because I did not know that someone who claimed to love me could so easily hurt me. I knew people could hurt me who did not love me, and I knew that people who loved me could hurt me and feel tremendous shame and regret about it. But I did not know that someone could claim to love me, hurt me violently, and then just go on with their life as if I did not matter. That was a new one for me. I guess spring is a time in which new things happen, even if those things are painful.

In the weeks that followed I walked about in a daze, alternating between suicidal ideations and a vast unnameable fatigue. I could not sleep because the panic attacks largely came in the middle of the night. I did all the things you're supposed to do in that situation, all the things I had learned were healthy responses to that kind of suffering. I exercised, talked with friends, prayed, joined in community, made myself of service to others who were in need, and spent a lot of time cleaning and working. I suspect all of it helped because I managed to survive whatever that was, and it might even be said that I recovered from it. I don't know how bad it could have gotten if I *hadn't* done any of those things, but I have some idea, and that is probably why I am alive today.

During those first few weeks, the cherry blossoms were the only things that gave me hope, as weird as that sounds. They didn't seem to care what I was going through. This was very important. My mind—which is another way of saying my entire existence—was consumed with my suffering. As far as I could tell, everything was my suffering. And yet here were these trees producing flowers that might turn to fruit almost as if the world had not opened up and been claimed by darkness. Imagine that. They were a reminder that no matter how bad things get or seem to get, there will be some kind of renewal, some kind of change. It may not be a change that you like, but whatever it will be, it will be different than what it is now. Sometimes that's all you can hope for.

I became obsessed with them. A particularly large and garish one dominated the sidewalk next to a church where I used to go to community meetings. I photographed it compulsively, working with angles and light and composition to try to capture, in some way, how glorious it is. I never could, of course. Cherry blossoms are basic in the way that god is basic—a beauty so fundamental that it cannot be consumed, owned, or captured. It can only be experienced, and even that only partially.

It had been fourteen years since my mother died. Right before she got diagnosed with the cancer that would ultimately kill her, she got really into gemstones. Many people who knew her, myself included if I'm being honest, wrote it off as the latest pointless obsession in a lifetime full of pointless obsessions. Not a lot of people respected my mother, I now realize. They all knew that she was brilliant, but everyone seemed to hold the opinion that she was somehow inconsequential, consumed as she was with shallow interests and what appeared to them as harebrained schemes never leading to anything important. She was not successful in the world of money or career; she was not good at things like keeping a roof over her head or food in the fridge. She never married, which I suspect some people saw as a failure. I've even heard it suggested that she was not a particularly good parent, which always seemed a bold thing to imply in a conversation with her only son.

Just recently someone said this to me about her: *She was very smart, your mother, but mentally she was not well put-together.* The funny thing about that sentence was it was clear to me that this person was actually trying to be careful. Like that was their version of protecting my feelings.

She is no longer here to defend herself or explain herself and I bet that's quite a relief for her. A lifelong swindler, she has pulled the ultimate grift on all of us by dying early and leaving us here to parse out what she actually meant. Now that she is an ancestor, I can only believe she knows fairly well how memory works, how it warps and undulates like the shimmering of heat, wrapping itself around our desires and fears, hopes and wounds. If you find some kind of self-justifying pleasure in thinking of her as a failure, then your memories will happily form around that. If you want to think of her as a work of genius, well, you can remember her that way too. In that way she is like nature: beautiful and messy, perpetually exposed and cosmically mysterious. Or maybe it's the way I love her that makes her so. Is there really a difference between the two?

God creates beautiful things so that we cannot understand them. I think that might be the entire point: to be in the humility of unknowing. The cherry blossoms have been captured on posters and calendars and tattoos and playing cards and animation forever. And still under the right circumstances, under the right amount of pain, the sight of one can literally save your life. We will never understand how or why that works, nor will we ever be able to capture it. That is god's flex. Beauty is meant to remind us that we can never fully understand all there is to understand. Beauty is meant to pleasantly put us all in our places.

The reason I like the gemstones, my mother once told me, *is that they hold all the secrets of the earth*. It's amazing, when you think about it, that she could find all the secrets of the earth on the Home Shopping Network. In moments like that she seemed to love the world in the same way we were taught that god loves us. By seeing the divine in every basic thing.

The Winner II

There is a photograph of me too.

I've looked at it only for a few moments at a time. Any longer and it is too intense. I am seven years old. I remember my age because I can remember every outfit I wore to picture day for every year that picture days were a thing. I even remember the outfit in my senior year, a year in which I made a game of avoiding picture day altogether. By then I was seventeen years old and the idea that it was not entirely appropriate for me to exist had firmly taken hold of me. Therefore, I was in no hurry to put on a suit and bow tie and sit down in front of a brown, abstract headshot backdrop and have my photo taken, with a stiff smile and my head tilted in some unnatural manner as directed by a weary school photographer. No, that would mean I was a real person who existed, who mattered, and the vast difference between this photographic truth and the truth of how I felt was enough to make my stomach knot up with fear. I didn't have the words for it then. But still, I knew it.

So I hid in a stairwell around the back of the school on picture day, listening to Jimi Hendrix, smoking cigarettes, and staring out at the smog that enveloped the San Gabriel Mountains. At the end of the year, when Ms. Castille, the yearbook adviser, realized I had not been photographed, she began to try to schedule a makeup shoot with me, at first kindly, and then with increasing annoyance. It became a kind of game for me. *Prove to me that I matter. I dare you.* Eventually she ambushed me in a hallway, hounded me into a classroom, and took a blurry shot of me against a blackboard. That was my senior portrait. I was wearing a vintage trench coat that I had tried with scissors and rudimentary sewing skills to fashion into some kind of blazer, the sleeveless Ocean Pacific shirt that had been a staple wardrobe item ever since I got it from the lost and found in ninth grade, and a vintage Pirates black pillbox hat with yellow stripes to remind me of my great-grandmother's house on the North Side of Pittsburgh, and its bedroom window through which I could watch the fireworks from Three Rivers Stadium lighting up the sky above the Heinz factory. I wanted that outfit to say everything I needed said about me. That I was fine with whatever. That I actually made *whatever* into something cool.

But the other photograph, the second-grade one, finds me in a tan waistcoat and matching pants, a brown plaid wide-collared shirt, and blue "The Winner II" sneakers from Sears that I knew didn't go with the outfit but that I loved and thought might miraculously work in a power-clashing kind of way. My mother had picked out the rest of the ensemble for me, and I felt it made me look like a dapper little man.

Those shoes were, for a brief moment, the most important thing I knew of in the entire world. I can still feel how the lightweight nylon and suede upper moved and scratched under my fingers when they were brand-new at the Sears at Landover Mall. They felt like a great expense for my mother, and she was pained paying for them— a grand gesture of how much it must hurt to love a child when you are poor. I tried to love the shoes enough to deserve them. I put them on and waited for their powers to take hold. Soon, I thought, the three white stripes on the side would activate, the light foam sole would engage, and my legs would be free of their limitations. If I ran fast enough in these, I believed, I could quite possibly fly. I didn't truly believe it. But then again, I did. This is how faith works for children. And we are all children.

When I look at that picture now, that picture of me in second grade, I don't see the "dapper," nor the "man." I just see the "little." I was so little. I look little in my eyes and in my face and in the defeated slump of my shoulders. I look little in the soft smile, somehow already exhausted and discontent. My hair is short, sloppily combed. I was hungry. I remember that about that day. I was hungry. Now I look into the eyes of that child, and I know that he already knows about the snow and the rising and falling of streetlamps. I know he knows about the razors and blood and how safety is just one room and one million light-years away. I look at that child and I know he has already been split into two. And I know that he knows how to put himself back together again because it is picture day, and it is much easier to smile and remain silent than it is to tell anyone the secrets he knows.

I can't locate that child in me anymore. He has been subsumed into all that I am, dissolved into my body like a teaspoon of salt into a cup of warm water. He is somewhere in here, in the body of a Black man with everything that means to the world: fear and murder and violence and the very worst of everyone's imagination. It is disorienting because that is so different from what it feels like on the inside, which is . . .

Well, I don't exactly know what it is. And that is the point. Because the other thing I know about that kid is that he already knows how to say "no" to anything he feels will make the people around him unhappy. Because he thinks that if the people around him are unhappy, then he is unsafe. If anyone is unhappy, then he will be taken by the snow and the ever-falling nights. He will belong to the razors and the quiet violence of Saturday mornings. He will belong to the pink hands turned shaking and white by the sheer angry and fearful force with which they grip the extended barrel of their LAPD-issued Sig Sauer P226 9mm.

What it feels like inside is everything. Rain and trees that reach to the sky, an ocean turned black by the night, the sliver of moon on granite, the lyrics to a song that keeps playing over and over in my head, the feeling that my entire skin is trembling every time Nina Simone hits that little climbing triplet run at the turnaround of the solo for "My Baby Just Cares for Me" and I throw my hands all the way up when she lands that triumphant final chord, a feeling that everything is on fire all the time and the quiet of the sky is the only thing that makes sense, a feeling that I am unsafe, deeply unsafe, everywhere I turn, everywhere I go, everything I do, I am in danger, a feeling that I am dangerous because I am in danger. I am too much, too big, too hairy, and too human.

I want to be held, but I want to feel safe. So often these two things don't work together.

A feeling that I am broken because these two things don't work together.

When my mother loved a song, she would write down the lyrics on a steno pad in Pitman shorthand that she learned at Strayer Secretarial College in the late 1970s. Then she would play the song over and over and over again, singing the lyrics, getting lost in that *feeling*. I would watch her, often in an empty living room because all the furniture had been sold or repossessed or put into storage and then sold when she couldn't pay the bill. I watched her spinning round and round in empty rooms, throwing her voice to the heavens, trying to climb there with her spirit. Sometimes I think it worked. Even as a child I was amazed at how sudden and intense her obsessions were. Until I learned that I am the very same way. It is as if our brains have been floating and bobbing in an interminable sea and they have finally found something to grab onto, and they will not, cannot, let go. We cling tight and fast until the tide pries us loose and sends us once again flinging into the emptiness. How she loved those moments of holding. How I loved seeing her have them.

At night I hold pillows. In the day I hold memories and dreams.

Always I hold that little boy in the picture. I hold his grief like a rosary. I hold it to remind him that he does not have to hold it alone. I am here now. He can be safe. He is now allowed to spend all his time and energy doing what he really loves: trying to run so fast and so far in his new shoes that he can finally fly.

They say you have to let go of the past in order to heal. But what if the past is now? Forever and ever now? What if by healing one moment, you can heal all the moments that ever were and ever are to come?

The Dog

When my son was about fourteen, he asked me what the best day of my life was. The question came from nowhere when we were driving down the freeway, on the way to get him some new shoes. This was a sacred mission for me because he almost never got new shoes. Of all his compulsive behaviors and his idiosyncrasies, this was one I found most surprisingly frustrating, how he wore the same pair of knit Adidas Boosts for like three of his teenage years and refused to change them. It made my feet hurt to look at him, it was like a form of torture he was enacting upon himself, and whenever I would confront him about it, he would just be like, "Why do I need new shoes, Dad, these are fine," and his toe would be poking out. One thing about your kids is that they will always find new and innovative ways, ways that you couldn't possibly have imagined, to stress you out.

His question about the best day of my life came out of nowhere because before that we had been sitting in silence. It shouldn't have been surprising because he was always asking questions like that, questions that made you realize he had been thinking about the meaning of things for a very long time, even when you thought he wasn't paying attention to anything. I gave it some consideration. "Of course," I told him, "the best days were the days you were born and your sister was born and the day I married your mother." And he was quiet for a little while before he said: "That's nice, Dad, but you always say that and that's a boring answer. What is the best day you ever had without us?"

I laughed a little. Looked out the window. And this day, the day I'm going to tell you about now, was the first one that popped into my mind. I did not know that it was the best day of my life until this very moment, so I'm glad he asked.

Maeve was a midwife. We had been friends, then lovers, then friends. She traveled a lot, sometimes for work—she was a midwife with Doctors Without Borders: the first of two such women with whom I'd be involved. I'm not sure what, if anything, to make of that small pattern. Sometimes she traveled for work, but other times she traveled for pleasure. She'd be in Colombia. Or France.

Or London. Or Tanzania. She was from an Irish family in a small town in New Jersey. She didn't talk much with her parents or her siblings, all of whom were driving kids around the suburbs in SUVs and buying big TVs. She was different from the people she grew up with. Sometimes she seemed like kind of a loner.

Once, when she was back in town for a few months and we were remembering to love each other again she said: *You should come with me to Mexico in October. Buy a ticket now.* She made travel decisions that way. Do it now. I did not make travel decisions that way. It seemed unreal to suddenly buy a ticket with no . . . I don't know . . . plan. But then I realized that a ticket is a plan. So, I bought one. In the car. From my phone. I guess I didn't want her to think I was scared. She was beautiful to me. But we had badly broken each other's hearts two years before, and we had been close but wary ever since.

In Mexico, we met in Oaxaca. And then flew in a tiny plane (Maeve called it a VW Bug with wings) down to a small beachfront town. We had a third person with us. Her name was Tyra. She was Maeve's friend from college. I had met Tyra once before in New York. She was slight and stunning and olive-skinned, skeptical with a curved back from scoliosis. She was born and raised in Queens by a white mother and a Jamaican father. She was both mousy and also appeared ready to fight anyone at any time. Whatever gentleness there was to her—and there was a fair amount—it seemed to me came from art and beauty. She was a painter, and it was easy to imagine that a studio was the only place on the planet where she felt completely safe. Like I said, she grew up in Queens. She wore large, formless brown and tan clothing that hid her thin frame and made her into a silhouette even when the sun shone directly on her.

We three slept in the same room, a small, hastily built guesthouse atop a set of treacherous stone stairs overlooking the beach. The toilet and shower were protected from the room only by a curtain that reached halfway to the floor. It was awkward whenever someone had to take a shit. It became a joke. We grew close. We lay awake at night singing R&B songs from our childhoods, talking about our fears. The moon was rising that week. The sea was outside our window. I was falling in love with both of them. It was fun being the only boy. The affections of women were like a religion to me. I thought they could sustain me for a long time.

On the fourth day, we decided to go to a beach on the other side of the ridge. We'd heard it was beautiful. Where we were was beautiful, but we were ready for a different beautiful. After swimming separately in the morning and meeting at a café for espresso and mangos and yogurt we set out. You had to walk halfway along the alley into town, an alley overrun with dogs, and German people with dreads, and the occasional plastic Coke bottle trodden over so often with sandals and motorcycles that it had become part of the earth. Past the houses and outdoor kitchens and heavy leaves on tin roofs, the smell of wood burning, a burro, a woman with an enormous belly and no teeth waving at you as you walk by.

You had to turn up this hill to get over the ridge, a

steep hill where you are talking when you start, but minutes into it you fall quiet. The sound of our three sets of feet on the dirt and gravel. The path led through canopies of trees and huts hidden from the road that looked vaguely ominous. At the top we reached a cemetery. It was midmorning. The cemetery was old, the headstones all colors, all faded. Flowers and the faces of the deceased hand-painted in soft pinks and baby blues, tattered banners hung from trees, clung to by dirt and cobwebs. We stood and watched until a dog emerged from the shadows behind a tombstone as if we had summoned it. He joined us and we continued walking. Now we were a foursome.

The beach was vast and straight and naked, unsheltered. Near-white sand seemingly spanned two miles in either direction from where we arrived. White flags could be seen placed at remarkably even intervals. We set out to walk the beach. We had not spoken in twenty minutes. We went forward in every combination. Me and Maeve. Maeve and Tyra. Tyra and the dog, whom we named Turtle the Dog. Turtle the Dog and me. For some moments we were all together, then the next moment, one of us would wander to the sea and stand before the waves, which loomed at terrifying heights and pounded the earth with the force of a bomb.

We came to the first white flag and realized it marked a sea turtle. The largest reptile I'd ever laid eyes on, largely decomposed, mostly dried, surrounded by a small cloud of sandflies. Its shell was halfway buried in the sand. Its massive flippers were almost reduced to bone. It

was as big as something in our human world. As big as
your table, or the desk at which I sit to write. It was big
enough to demand an entire seat on an airplane or bus.
Turtle the Dog sniffed around. That's why we would
name him Turtle the Dog. Tyra and I warned him to stay
away as if he were our child. We examined it for a while
then moved on.

We continued to another white flag, and it marked
another turtle. We realized that someone had planted
white flags at the site of every turtle carcass. This one
even further decomposed. Nearly sun-bleached. The
enormous shell was so perfectly appointed with polygon
spirals, each a small pyramid, each a layer of years and
years. Maeve and Turtle the Dog had drifted down the
beach to play fetch. I could see them as shadows against
the sun, the glow of the wet sand, his body jumping and
contorting with excitement, her body running and playing like a child.

Tyra wanted to see what was under the shell and suddenly I had a purpose. I went to find the biggest stick I
could, a branch so heavy I could only drag it back, leaving a long trail in the sand. I began to pry the shell off.
Never before had I felt so useful. I approached it from
angles, I formulated plans, I calculated resistance. I got
another log and created leverage. And I pried and pried.
Tyra watched me, her hands on her hips, which were
thrust forward. Her brown bony back curved like an S. I
wanted to make this happen so badly for her that I almost began to cry. I wanted to give this to her. I almost
cry now thinking about it. I don't know why. Maybe

everything is worth crying over if you spend enough time with it.

Eventually I got the shell off and Maeve joined us. She explained its anatomy. She knew a lot about the inside of bodies. We listened. Turtle the Dog chased birds.

I walked to the water and watched. Seven years before that, I took my mother's ashes to the sea, after she died in my arms. I felt her presence, the first time since that day. I cried in a way that didn't matter because of the spray of the sea, because of the force of the wind. To be ten feet from someone on a beach like that is to be a mile from them. It is like a tundra. I felt at home there.

We had seen enough dead turtles. The sun seemed to have moved so we started back without saying anything. Trudging through the sand, swerving into one another and away again. It seemed both longer and shorter before we arrived at a hut near the path that had dumped us off on the beach. There was a bar, but it was closed. A young man was moving buckets of ice around. We asked if he would serve us, and he agreed. Maeve and Tyra had Bohemias. I had Coke in a bottle. He brought out three bamboo deck chairs and we sat in them and looked out at the sea. Tyra looked so much like herself with a beer in her hand and her eyes on the horizon.

Evening fell. Slowly. Like something we forgot could happen.

After nightfall I was standing at the water. Maeve was in the chair, back by the bar. Turtle the Dog was dozing by her feet. Tyra was sticking her toes in the water, close to me but not close enough for us to be doing it together.

I saw bioluminescence. A spot in the sea lit up like god was winking at me. I didn't believe it. I waited for it to happen again before I told Tyra. It did. She came over and stood right next to me. We stared into the darkness of the sea, but we saw nothing. I did not know if it was true. Tyra told me she believed me. Then it happened again! She squealed. And then one more time! A sudden flash of light right under the water of our feet! My arm was around her now. Her head was in the crook of my chest. Her hair smelled of sweat and cocoa. I kissed her hair. I felt her sigh, but could not hear it. We stood this way for what seemed like not long enough.

I looked back to see what Maeve was doing. She was walking back up the path into the darkness by herself. We called out. She told us she was leaving. We asked her to wait. She didn't want to. Turtle the Dog couldn't figure out who to side with. Tyra and I felt like we had been caught doing something we should not. We hastily gathered ourselves and joined her on the path. We never spoke of it again.

It was dark. Turtle the Dog snorted along beside us. Underneath the trees we could not see our hands. To ward off the fear we talked about eighties TV shows. We talked about turtles. We climbed the hill, our breath the only sound. Everything seemed longer, darker than before. When we arrived at the crest, we realized we were at the cemetery again. We could make out the shadows of a bird perched atop a tombstone. After a moment, Turtle the Dog peeled off from our group, trotted into the cemetery, and disappeared once again among the graves.

Soon we could no longer hear his paws. Soon we could no longer hear his breathing. Soon we were alone.

Halfway down the hill, we rounded a bend and the whole of the village and the valley was spread out before us. Piles of hills and houses and above it all in the middle of the sky, a bold, pregnant, crying full moon was rising slowly from behind a bank of thick clouds. We were all watching it. The whole earth. A few bats flew over it for effect. It was October. The air was growing cool in the evening. We stood in the middle of the road and watched the moon give birth to itself. Others would pass by and stop to silently join our group. Sometimes a person would whistle. Sometimes they'd say nothing, just smile at us before they moved on. When the show was over, and the moon risen, we descended into town.

We walked to a restaurant, a pizza place with no walls under a tin roof. We had been there before. We were on a smiling-and-nodding basis with the people who worked there. The moon was fully up now, and no one was in the restaurant. The entire staff and the cooks were all standing in the street, their faces tilted toward the sky and kitchen towels slung over their shoulders. We stood with them and looked up too. The radio was playing a live version of Elvis Presley singing "Are You Lonesome Tonight?" His voice quavered and reverbed seemingly all the way to the heavens. We stood. Maeve. Tyra. Me. The waitress. The cooks. Another customer. Another dog.

No one moved until the song was over.

The Rain

I used to wonder what I was going to do at the end of the world and then I realized that every day is at the end of the world. We are not pre-apocalyptic. We are mid-apocalyptic, or perhaps peri-apocalyptic. When have we not been? When have we not decimated life, filled the skies with fire, the rivers with blood? There have been times when that hasn't been happening but there was not human time before that was happening.

But the apocalypse I am living through, like most things, does not look like they told me it would look. I am not confronted with roving bands of cannibals or people wearing human skulls as jewelry. Our apocalypse is slow and steady, with plenty of water breaks and scenic pauses.

I think I love you.

Everything makes more sense to me when I think of it this way, as an ending. It is endings I know and understand best and I think this helps me understand life because life is all endings. From the moment I stepped into the fog I've been facing endings and voids and the threats of long, empty abysses.

At a certain point I knew what I would be doing when things ended. I would be paying attention. I would be fully living and trying to love to the very ends of my grasp, the limits of myself. I would take each moment as a miracle. I would see everything there was to see, holding my face, my body to the fires of love. I would try.

I noticed recently that almost all animals have the same eyes, birds and lizards, whales and leopards, roaches and frogs and rodents and jaguars. Black. Infinite. Ancient. Without hurry or pause. Without judgment or deception. I wonder if this might be the eye of god.

I wonder if this simple and pure way of seeing is, in fact, another word for love.

We celebrated the rains when they first began. *Finally,* we said, *isn't it beautiful?* We had been freed from the grasp of fire season, the stasis of suffocation, the threat of burning. We put out our plants and took videos of cute finches sheltering on our windowsills. We heard there was a river in the sky, an atmospheric river. We had known that we could be on a river, or in a river, but were only recently coming to understand that we could be beneath one too.

Then the rains we had called for refused to stop. Flash flood warnings were in effect. The places where the earth had been scarred by fire were now the most vulnerable to being washed away by flood. The cycle continued. The wind banged our doors, rattled our windows. Trees undulated, bent and snapped. It was a Sunday. They were still playing football. They were still hawking barbecue grills and all-new SUVs and cell phones and crunchy, cheesy snacks. The emergency before had been not enough rain. Now the emergency was too much.

We tried to create vibes. We burned incense and candles. We made soups, posted memes, scrolled and scrolled all the way into infinity. The doors rattled, the windows banged, the tree branches snapped and collapsed, ending electricity until it could be repaired, which it was, until it could be ended again. We texted our friends, we watched our friends on Insta, we thought about friends we hadn't spoken to in far too long, we dreamt of friends we never had, we became our only friends, we became alone.

We built a little, but the sky was a lot.

We heard the ceaseless churning, swaying and running, clattering and collapsing, and we called it weather. We only knew of it as weather, weather was all our brains had been trained to understand. Weather was temporary. Weather could be waited out. The origins of weather had nothing to do with us, we were not responsible for weather. Our only task with weather was to deal with it, to put on the proper gear and tough it out.

But this was not weather, this was change—a thing we understood entirely less of. We did not remember change, we did not remember its disrobing, its unhinging, its deboning. We did not remember its dismantling, its disconnecting, its destabilizing. We did not remember that it was death that creates the life force of change, that change must kill things, that change must break things open to heal what has been sickened and closed. We did not remember that the rain was water and that water washes and sweeps and wears everything away. Everything away. Even the mountains.

We celebrated the rains when they first began.

We feared change because we knew change would hurt. We held on doggedly to Things as They Have Always Been even though Things as They Have Always Been was what had caused the sickening in the first place! We were in a catch-22, a spiral, a hurricane, a bomb cyclone. We tried to grasp it, and it was like trying to grasp the rain in our fists. We looked, instead, for something we could grasp, and we found guns and pets. We found plants and selfies. We found outrage and TikToks. We found burritos and protests. We found jobs and the quitting of jobs. We found Octavia Butler and *Breath of the Wild*. We found cancellation and rebirth. We found squash recipes and new nail colors, dalgona coffee and Crocs. We found each other. We found each other everywhere we looked, even and most especially within ourselves. We braved the rain to find each other, the light waves. The freeways and fires. We walked across the flames and under the rivers, we pushed the oceans to the side to find each other. We held hands and kissed on foreheads and did not know what to say to each other so it was nothing that we said.

We celebrated the rains when they first began. They were unlike the fog that had blocked us from seeing, unlike the snow that had frozen us out, made us huddle and hide. The rains made things clear, clean, and new again. Just as they always were. The rains came to cleanse.

It is the end of everything, which is another way of saying it is the beginning of everything. It is the end of the day, which is to say it is the beginning of the stars and the beams of moonlight bathing the chuparosas and the ponderosa pines. It is the end of isolation, which is another way of saying it is the beginning of the embrace in which we mourn and wail, love and weep. It is the end of supremacy, which is another way of saying it is the beginning of calling one another on the wind, our poems carried like pollen from one clump of us to another.

How long have we labored under the shadow of this death, this murder of the earth, of the spirit, of one another? It seems we have done so forever, but it hasn't even been one-millionth of the time upon which the ocean has had waves. This floundering, abusive nation is as small in time as an apple is upon the entirety of the earth. And yet like the ocean, this abuse seems to go on forever.

What must die within you to free us? What do we have to let end to be born?

I used to write alone. Always alone. *I can't hang out,*

I would tell my friends. *I have to go write.* My phone on do not disturb, websites blocked, curtains drawn, emails unanswered, door closed. Lately I have been feeling just the opposite, like I cannot write alone. I need to write with the sunlight on my face surrounded by people I love. I need to be with my friends, I need hugs and cookies and afternoon tea. I am writing a future, after all. What sense does it make to write it without you?

I am thinking about how in 2020 it took us three months of staying home from work before we agreed that it was time for the largest protests in the history of the country. Three months. I'm thinking about how much time it takes to survive in capitalism, how much energy. How we have to look for healthcare and parking, stand in line at the returns desk, figure out how to pay rent, post our businesses online in the hopes that someone will pay us for our work. How we have to care for dying parents, and our children alone, how we have to recover from grief, mourn the dead, those who did nothing to deserve their murders, how we have to fight for recognition, humanity, how we have to plead to be taken seriously, treated as human beings under our own human systems. I think about how isolating it can all be, how no one wants to lose what little they have in order to help someone else because even though you have nothing, at least you have something.

I think about the spiritual, emotional, psychic toll of all of this and how we are *struggling mentally, spiraling, staring into the void*, watching the days blow away like so much sand. And I think about the winds that rattle the foundations of the house I'm sitting in, reminding me that a mere breath from the earth can send me and all of us rocketing into eternity.

It all makes me think of how fragile we are. Which is good news. This means that everything that we've created can crumble. The police. The governments. The tanks and rockets. The systems, the hierarchies, the castles made upon sand, violence, the murders. In bedrooms and schoolrooms, on playgrounds, in grocery stores, in deserts, and alleyways, and homes, and offices. All of it can crumble. All of it can be reborn. It must. We must. This is another way of saying *love*.

Postscript

A Story About Dill

The Dill

For a person who claims to understand endings I
have a notoriously hard time knowing when to stop writing. To that end, I have just one more story to tell:

The three of us had been snacking for the better part of
the early afternoon, filling a table with everything we
could carry. Crackers both fancy and Goldfish, multiple
cheeses, winter mandarins, two kinds of smoked salmon,
smoked cod, chocolate, three kinds of chips, and an exceedingly mediocre store-bought hummus that we tried
and failed to spruce up with lemon, smoked paprika, garlic, and salt.

One of us mentioned offhandedly that she always
keeps dill and parsley in her fridge and that she makes a

thing with it that she described as having only a few in-
gredients and being able to go on anything. *Hm . . .
maybe I'll make it*, she said, getting up from the table and
heading into the kitchen. It was my first time meeting
her. She was a friend of a friend, but I knew her a little
from online. She used to run an inspirational food nonprofit that I saw stories about in local news. It shuttered
during the pandemic. She was now working as a costume
designer on a TV show shooting locally.

She located a salad spinner (it was not her kitchen)
and took out an unusually large and verdant bunch of
Italian flat-leaf parsley. I watched as she separated each
strand of parsley, briefly inspecting it and setting aside
the less-than-acceptable ones while she told us the story
of her trip to her mother's homeland.

She described rocky, failing roads, bumpy pickup
trucks, small villages where the women looked so much
like her mother that it brought her to tears. A village el-
der who spoke no English and lived in a tiny shelter that
he shared with his livestock, into which he invited her to
drink and laugh at the bare table. She was the guest of
honor.

I watched as she worked over the herbs. After she had
reduced the pile by about 5 percent by taking out the
slightly wilted ones, she began to take the leaves from
the stalk. Individually. There was no hurry to the way
she worked, nor was there speed. She peeled each leaf as
if we had all day to peel leaves. We did not. But it was
then that I realized that we did.

I found myself mesmerized with the slowness. If I am

ever tasked with making something out of herbs, my method is to rinse them, chop them, throw them into the dish, and then move on to the next thing. My mind kept stuttering over the fact that she was taking so long, almost as if there were something wrong with how long she was taking, though I could not name what it was.

Her story had become funny. Something about finding a poster of a shirtless Kanye wearing a gold cross in a remote and unlikely place in her family's village. We were laughing. She had done such a good job of painting the characters in the story that when I think back on that moment it seems odd that there were only three of us in the room. I seem to remember there being dozens of us, a whole dinner party, in fact. She moved on to the dill, repeating the same process: rinsing, drying, picking over, peeling each leaf with painstaking attention.

Now she was describing a feast that was made for her. Her visit had coincided with the celebration of a local baby. Where her people are from, she explained, it is forbidden to see the baby before it has survived for ninety days. She happened to arrive to the village on the baby's ninetieth day and relatives from near and far had come to celebrate these twin blessings. The alcohol was flowing. There was laughter and music. She thought the food would be presented in some formal way at some point, but she soon learned that the food just kept coming. Dish after dish after dish after dish. Everything was delicious. *The thing is*, she explained, fiddling with and then fixing the salad spinner, which had gone off the track, *it's considered rude to have any part of the table that doesn't have food on it. So, like if there's, like, even a space this big*—and here she took her hands from the fresh, wet dill and demonstrated a shape roughly the size of a small paperback book—*someone will, like, put a lemon wedge or some leaves on a dish just to fill up that space.* It was here that I noticed how the fuchsia of her nails made gorgeous asymmetry with the green of the dill.

Soon she was mixing the herbs in a small bowl with salt and olive oil and red pepper flakes. Considering the labor that had gone into it, the final product struck me as a remarkably small amount of food. I found myself once again trying to understand where this constant measure of efficiency and output was coming from inside me. It was a Saturday. We were ostensibly on a mini vacation. I did not have a place to be, nor a time to be there. I tried to imagine working this slowly in my home kitchen and I could not. I love cooking. I seem to be good at cooking. But lately cooking had become a means to an end, a short work break that also makes it possible for me to eat, a thing that makes a mess and takes up time, a thing that I'd have to wrap up quickly so I could get back to work. It occurred to me that this person was treating the preparing of food as the meal in and of itself.

I just like it, she explained as if reading my thoughts, *because when I was little this is all my mother and aunts would let me do.* "Take the leaves off the herbs," *they would say.* "Take the leaves off the herbs." *So when I smell these herbs, it reminds me of them.*

She took a few more tastes, made a few more adjustments. When she was done, we each scooped a little spoonful of the stuff onto toasted rye bread with some smoked fish on it. It was good. Not mind blowing. Just good. Very good. Good enough that I thought about it that night when I went to bed and in the morning when I woke up. Good enough that I wrote about it. Good enough that I decided to remember that it happened.

It is nearly Lunar New Year, when the night sky is unlit by the moon, the one period of time in which you can rest from your work in the fields. So, you use it to join with the people you love. You come to them and they to you with gifts. You bring joy to them. You hope for good blessings.

My good blessing this new year has been story and a pair of hands that touched each leaf as if each leaf were a loving living thing, as if I deserved to eat things that had been loved in this way.

In the quiet of the new moons, in the cold of the nights wherever you are, I hope you know that you too deserve to eat things that have been loved in this way, to hear stories in which each word, each sentence has been caressed in the luminescent glow of afternoon sunlight, trimmed and lacquered in sparkling fuchsia.

I hope you know that you deserve that, and that each of us, from times before we were even born, always has.

Acknowledgments

Jim Rutman, Sean McDonald, Danny Vazquez, Rodrigo Corral, for helping make this book a reality. The whole team at FSG × MCD. Benjamin Brooks for telling me it mattered.

Red H., Algiin F., John V., Harvey A., Skyler, Norman, Johnny, Abbe, Lara, Michelle M., Lakeside 10, Rockridge Fellows, thanks for letting me be of service.

LACHSA for teaching me work. 245 Varet and ETW for teaching me creation. Jean and Bill Harvey for support, mentorship, room and board.

Jessica Hopper for wisdom, Nina Aaron for clarity, A. M. Darke for light, Simone Harvey for wisdom. Emily McDowell for beaches and decades. Darcie Vigliano for fellowship of the spirit, Shana Lancaster for kitchens and clothes. Penne for your Thots. Siena Meeks for movies and talks. Therapy and Chill, Maura Darrow for mental health and pie. Noleca and Homero Radway for infinite homes. Naushon Kabat-Zinn for latkes and laughs, Maura Daly for couches and playlists. Amanda Machado for voice notes and adventures, Sara Beladi for pomodoros and fishnets. POC Queergasm Club. Celeste Cooper for home and scones. Sheila Menezes for smuggling me into my only writing course. Beto Palomar, my P4P student teacher poet. Yeshi forever. Aminta forever.

Some people who have helped me believe in myself as a writer: Hanif Abdurraqib, Riz Ahmed, Jordan Bailey, Sadie Barnette, Alexander Chee, Nicole Cliffe, Eve Ewing, Melissa Febos, Ashley C. Ford, Essence Harden, Morgan Jerkins, Saeed Jones, Donika Kelly, Porochista Khakpour, Kiese Laymon, Alexis Madrigal, Melina Matsoukas, James McBride, Tarell Alvin McCraney, Casey Miner, Morgan Parker, Jennifer Pastiloff, Danzy Senna, Doreen St. Félix, Rudy Thomas, Ed Vaverick, Lena Waithe.

Some editors who have taught me the craft: Nitsuh Abebe, Julie Caine, Christopher Cox, Leila Day, Justin Ellis, Dan Fierman, Leah Flickinger, David Haglund, David Hainey, Jessica Hopper, Dee Lockett, Jessica Lustig, Dani McClain, Casey Miner, Lindsay Peoples Wagner, Jessica Reed, Simon Vozick-Levinson.

T. Mariquita for love and honey. We have already lived forever. May we be eternally blessed.

The fam who held me: Tausha, Lee Lee, CJ, Red, Shirley, Beverly, Gertie, Carvell, Melvin, William, Lessie, Chrissie, Bernice, Al, Wilabelle, Bea.

Pops for teaching me how to ask questions and appreciate life.

Resham for loving.

Jo for decades of life.

I'd like to thank myself for surviving and following the poetry.

Extra special thanks to The Kids for running through the fields, growing up beautifully, taking my money, seeing me truly, loving me honestly. My Heroes.

June Jordan for showing me how to be what god made me.

Finally, Parthenia: for carrying me, breathing life into me, and showering me in laughter and gemstones.

A Note About the Author

Carvell Wallace grew up between southwestern Pennsylvania, Washington, DC, and Los Angeles. He attended the New York University Tisch School of the Arts and worked as a stage actor before spending fifteen years in direct-service youth non-profits. He has covered art, entertainment, music, culture, race, sports, and parenting for *The New York Times Magazine*, *The New Yorker*, *Slate*, *GQ*, *Pitchfork*, MTV News, and other outlets. As a podcast host, he has been nominated for a Peabody Award and won a Kaleidoscope Award. He is the coauthor of Andre Iguodala's *New York Times* bestselling basketball memoir *The Sixth Man*. He lives in Oakland and has two adult children, a comfortable couch, and a lot of plants.